Just in Time:
Moments in Teaching Philosophy

Just in Time: Moments in Teaching Philosophy

A Festschrift Celebrating the Teaching of James Conlon

Edited by
JENNIFER HOCKENBERY DRAGSETH

☙PICKWICK *Publications* • Eugene, Oregon

JUST IN TIME: MOMENTS IN TEACHING PHILOSOPHY
A Festschrift Celebrating the Teaching of James Conlon

Copyright © 2019 Wipf and Stock Publishers. All rights reserved. Except for brief quotations in critical publications or reviews, no part of this book may be reproduced in any manner without prior written permission from the publisher. Write: Permissions, Wipf and Stock Publishers, 199 W. 8th Ave., Suite 3, Eugene, OR 97401.

Pickwick Publications
An Imprint of Wipf and Stock Publishers
199 W. 8th Ave., Suite 3
Eugene, OR 97401

www.wipfandstock.com

PAPERBACK ISBN: 978-1-5326-5471-8
HARDCOVER ISBN: 978-1-5326-5472-5
EBOOK ISBN: 978-1-5326-5473-2

Cataloguing-in-Publication data:

Names: Hockenbery Dragseth, Jennifer, editor.

Title: Just in time: moments in teaching philosophy: a festschrift celebrating the teaching of James Conlon / edited by Jennifer Hockenbery Dragseth.

Description: Eugene, OR: Pickwick Publications, 2019 | Includes bibliographical references.

Identifiers: ISBN 978-1-5326-5471-8 (paperback) | ISBN 978-1-5326-5472-5 (hardcover) | ISBN 978-1-5326-5473-2 (ebook)

Subjects: LCSH: Conlon, James, 1948–. | Philosophy—Studying and teaching.

Classification: B52.T38 2019 (print) | B52.T38 (ebook)

Manufactured in the U.S.A.   FEBRUARY 11, 2019

Contents

Contributors | vii
Foreword by Jennifer Hockenbery Dragseth | ix
Preface by Celcy Powers-King | xi

Section I. Passionate Moments: Teaching about Desire | 1
    An Aesthetic Reading of Sexual Sounds *by James Conlon* | 3
    Pornophony *by Maggie Ann Labinski* | 13

Section II. Transformative Moments: Teaching Philosophy's Relevance | 29
    Stanley Cavell and the Predicament of Philosophy
        by James Conlon | 31
    Worlds Worth Wanting *by Anne M. Maloney* | 42

Section III. Effable Moments: Teaching the Power of Writing | 55
    Against Ineffability *by James Conlon* | 57
    Defining the Terms of Surrender *by Austin M. Reece* | 79

Section IV. Pragmatic Moments: Just Teaching in America | 95
    Cornel West's Socratic Understanding of America
        by James Conlon | 97
    Doing *Just* Philosophy *by Marsha Thrall* | 116

Section V. Temporal Moments: Teaching in Time | 125
    Before Sunset and the Truth of Time *by James Conlon* | 127
    Just in Time *by Jennifer Hockenbery Dragseth* | 138

Contributors

James Conlon is professor emeritus of philosophy at Mount Mary University where he taught from 1974–2017. He currently lives in New York City with his wife Mary.

Jennifer Hockenbery Dragseth is professor of philosophy at Mount Mary University where she has taught since 1998.

Maggie Ann Labinski is assistant professor of philosophy at Fairfield University. She graduated with majors in philosophy, theology, and English from Mount Mary University in 2003.

Anne Maloney is associate professor of philosophy at Saint Catherine's University. She graduated with a major in philosophy from Mount Mary University in 1980.

Celcy Powers King is a philosophy major at Mount Mary University and the editorial assistant for this volume. She will graduate in 2019.

Austin M. Reece is a lecturer in philosophy at Mount Mary University where he has taught since 2007. He is a doctoral candidate in philosophy at Dublin City University.

Marsha Thrall graduated from Mount Mary University with majors in philosophy and theology in 2012. Currently she is a doctoral candidate in the Religion, Ethics and Society Program at Chicago Theological Seminary.

Foreword
JENNIFER HOCKENBERY DRAGSETH, EDITOR

WHEN DR. JAMES CONLON came to Mount Mary College (now University) it was 1974. He was 26 years old. It is worth noting that Conlon had already taught junior high in the bayou country of Louisiana, driven a school bus, obtained a Ph.D. in philosophy at Marquette University, married his life-long wife, and fathered his first daughter. Conlon joined Drs. George McMullen and John Carmichael in a department housed behind the sacristy of Notre Dame Hall. In the 1970s, he was the baby, and the babe, of the group. In fact, the story goes that when the students asked Conlon on the first day of class what he wanted to be called, he said, being young and hip, "You may call me whatever you think is best." The leader of the class said "Okay, Baby." As Conlon says, Mount Mary has always had bold women. In the 43 years that he served at Mount Mary, many other professors came and went. Deans, provosts, and presidents came and went. Conlon stayed; he is a loyal intellectual in an age that does not always value loyalty. In that time, he taught philosophy to over 4000 women in 250 different classes. Because few colleges today require philosophy classes for students who are not philosophy majors and because few philosophy majors are women, the impact of Jim's career of teaching philosophy to women is uniquely large. Mount Mary was and is an urban, Catholic institution of higher education for women. The majority of the women whom the University serves are women from working class backgrounds who are usually targeted for professional and vocational training rather than a liberal arts education. Conlon's career has been one of advocacy and support for women from diverse backgrounds to engage in the pleasures and practices of philosophy. To do this well, Conlon had to be an excellent teacher and to advocate for the pursuit of excellent teaching.

This book is a celebration of his philosophical ideas and his pedagogical practices with the aim to encourage others who teach and learn in philosophy. Each section pairs an academic paper of Conlon's with a reflection by a former student or colleague that discusses the same idea and then puts Conlon's philosophy into the context of teaching and learning. In the section, Passionate Moments: Teaching about Desire, Conlon's provocative essay on the aesthetics of listening to sexual sounds is paired with Maggie Labinski's own feminist consideration of the question especially in the context of teaching contemporary undergraduates. In the section, Transformative Moments: Teaching Philosophy's Relevance, Conlon's important insights on how philosophy of film can bridge the chasm between academic philosophers and the public are echoed by Anne Maloney's reflections on teaching her undergraduates about the necessity and dangers of studying philosophy through watching and analyzing films. The third section, Effable Moments: Teaching the Power of Writing, pairs Conlon's beautiful essay against the lazy plea of ineffability with Austin M. Reece's own reflection about the difficult but healing art of making traumatic experience effable. In the fourth section, Pragmatic Moments: Just Teaching, Conlon's work on American philosopher Cornel West is followed by Marsha Thrall's discussion of the need to teach the call for social justice. The final section of the book, Temporal Moments: Teaching in Time pairs an essay of Conlon's about the nature of time with my discussion of what Conlon's view might mean specifically for teaching and learning.

This volume is a work of love: for James Conlon, for Mount Mary University, for the discipline and passion of Philosophy. All of the contributors hope that this volume will inspire others who teach and learn in philosophy to make use of each moment of wonder in the classroom and in life as they pursue new insights together with their students and colleagues. We thank our own families, students, and institutions for their help as we pursued the ideas in this book and strove for effability so that we might share them with others.

Preface

CELCY POWERS-KING, EDITOR'S ASSISTANT

As a student at Mount Mary University, I have had the wonderful opportunity to be a student of James Conlon twice. Both experiences significantly impacted my decision to become a philosophy major and to explore where philosophy could take me. When I first entered Mount Mary as a freshman I was an Interior Design major. I thought I knew what I wanted in life; I thought I was very self-aware; I knew what interested me and what I valued. I soon learned that I had little to no idea of what I really wanted in life or who I was. However, through Dr. Conlon's classes, I discovered new truths about myself and the value philosophy holds for everyone.

My first experience as Dr. Conlon's student took place in a course he instructed called Philosophy of Love. In this course, we examined conceptions of love, the value of love, and other related topics such as the influence on love of sexual intercourse and sexuality. The conversations that surrounded these topics frequently gave Dr. Conlon the opportunity to critique a student's position or argument in an effort to help her evolve and structure her own ideas. The most important thing Dr. Conlon taught me as a philosopher is the ability to structure a good argument. At times it was vexing to be stumped by his line of questioning, especially when I thought I knew what I was talking about. But, a philosophy teacher may not be really doing his job if he does not encourage an existential life crisis as his student tries to figure out what her words really mean. In so doing, the role Dr. Conlon played in our philosophy classes enabled us to analyze critically our own thoughts and ideas.

Now that I am almost at the end of my journey as an undergraduate student, I have come to realize that the philosophical conversations Dr. Conlon engaged with me have become some of the most meaningful conversations I have ever had. The value of teaching philosophy is immense. To understand the value in teaching philosophy is to cherish the value of education. Wisdom is what we gain from education, and that wisdom is what enables us to change ourselves and the world around us. The value of teaching philosophy is that in so doing the professor gives any student willing to learn the tools to look at the world in a new light, protect herself from unjustified authority, fight questionable values, and dismantle unfounded beliefs.

Teaching philosophy is important because of its pursuit of timeless values like truth, justice and wisdom. These timeless truths are always relevant, deepening our understanding of our own human experiences in time. For example, there will never be a time, in time, in which we no longer need the ideal of justice to guide us as we develop society. A philosophical education is our path to understand what Justice is. As such, education is one of the few things that can never be stolen once it is obtained.

More personally, without studying philosophy I have no idea what kind of person I would now be. If I never had the opportunity to study philosophy formally, I would have never learned the value of therapy in particular. Indeed, philosophy introduced me to therapy by introducing me to the importance of analyzing thought patterns from different perspectives. Philosophy encourages students to ask questions of others in regards to their values; I started doing that to myself. Initially I had to ask myself if I had value as a person and what constitutes my value. Soon I was using philosophy as therapy to help me cope with everyday life and each wild journey I encountered as a young adult. By this, I mean that I used philosophy as a means to heal through reason.

Personally, I needed to heal from feelings of worthlessness because I was grieving the loss of what I thought was my self. Reason helped me dispel sources of false worthlessness and helped me evaluate what I had lost. I realized that I had not really lost my self but I had lost previously satisfying definitions of my self. I was holding myself to standards that no longer supported who I was becoming. Life is a learning process; I learned to continuously work on matters of self development as I wanted to heal from events that caused me harm. Ultimately healing through reason is my attempt to alleviate negative feelings through logic. This is one of the greatest assets I have learned to use in my life. This grew from Dr. Conlon's rigorous lines of questioning that taught me never to stop asking questions until I come to an answer that is valid and satisfactory. Philosophy came just in time for me.

SECTION I

Passionate Moments
Teaching about Desire

An Aesthetic Reading of Sexual Sounds[1]
JAMES CONLON

IN THIS ESSAY, I analyze the experience of overhearing sounds of sexual pleasure in strangers. While the experience is not something that happens everyday, and there are probably some people for whom it has never happened, it is, I believe, a common enough experience, a memorable enough experience, to serve as a meaningful object of analysis. The circumstances and scenarios for this experience are as strange and as normal as human beings themselves, but the one Paul Simon recounts in his song "Duncan" (1974) is fairly typical and will serve as a way to focus my analysis. The song is the story of Lincoln Duncan, a boy setting out from home for the first time, who overhears a couple making love in the motel room next to his. Their sounds move him to reflect on his upbringing and his own first sexual experience. These reflections become the creative source of the song he sings.

As in Duncan's case, the experience I have in mind is ordinarily not sought.[2] It is, rather, something that happens serendipitously, a contingent by-product of being in a particular place at a particular time. For example, Duncan lands in this particular cheap motel purely by happenstance. The sounds from the couple in the next room arrive entirely unplanned.

But even though the sounds are unsought, they are not, in the end, unchosen. There are surely ways Duncan could reject the "noise" (by turning up his radio, for example, or knocking on the wall). But there is some

---

1. This paper was previously published in *International Journal of Sexuality and Gender Studies* 7 (2002) 51–59. It is reprinted in this volume by permission from Springer.

2. I do not want to exclude the possibility that sexual sounds be sought out specifically for aesthetic purposes—by bugging a particular bedroom, for example. Such activities, however, would usually involve motives other than the aesthetic, and be far from the "everyday life" experience I have in mind.

Section I—Passionate Moments

point when the hearer chooses the sounds, welcomes them as part of her own experience. That there is such a point for Duncan is confirmed by the fact of the song itself, which is intentionally being composed and sung against the backdrop of the sounds he is hearing.

It is also important that the sounds be not just heard, but overheard. My analytic interest here is not the experience of art, but that area called the aesthetics of everyday life. In other words, the sexual sounds I am concerned with originate in the context of a real life intimacy assumed by the participants to be private; if the sounds are consciously performed before an audience, they lose a crucial part of their meaning. This applies, I would argue, to the recent internet phenomenon of websites that offer 24-hour access to a person's room or apartment. Although the actions at such sites are "real life" in the sense that they are not structured toward an artistic purpose, they are inevitably influenced by the participants' knowledge of their public exposure. Thus, although unscripted and unrehearsed, they would count as a "performance" in some sense and be excluded from my focus. Essential to the aesthetic excitement of my hearer is her presence as a "fly on the wall," an interloper on someone else's intimacy.

Another crucial aspect of the experience I have in mind is that it be exclusively auditory. To include sight would complicate the experience in ways that would not be helpful to my analysis. It would threaten, for example, the distance necessary for the experience to be truly aesthetic. The seer has practical worries about being seen, being discovered, that the hearer does not have. Also, sight is a more sensually involving sense, a less contemplative one, than hearing. Sight is more the utilized tool for a sexual arousal that would conflict with the aesthetic.

In choosing to emphasize the aesthetic, however, I do not want to detract from the powers of sound for sexual arousal. The sexual sounds of others are often a stimulus to one's own sexual arousal. But without denying the power sexual sounds have to cause sexual pleasure, I claim that they also have the power to cause aesthetic pleasure, to move us by the meaning and intensity of their beauty.

It is my interest in isolating the aesthetic of these sounds that leads me to focus on strangers. I am well aware that families, especially extended families, provide all sorts of opportunities for overhearing the sounds of sexual activities of their members. This is especially true in cultures and classes that have less access to privacy than middle-class families in modern, industrial society. The psychological complexities, however, surrounding sexual matters within families would needlessly complicate my task and again detract from its aesthetic focus.

Freud often noted the developmental significance of the child's sight of parental sex, what he called "the primal scene."[3] Whatever one thinks about the details of Freudian theory, children do sometimes witness, either through sight or sound, parental sex. Also, adolescents do sometimes include family members in aspects of their burgeoning fantasy life.[4] I am convinced that some of the emotional power present in overhearing sexual sounds, even in strangers, is the resonance and relevance they have to the hearer's own psychosexual history. But when the sounds of sexual pleasure are from family members and are, in some loose sense, "incestuous," the experience becomes quite complex and makes isolating its aesthetic qualities highly problematic. This is why I choose to focus on the sexual sounds of those outside the family; strangers or minimal acquaintances.

I need to make one final clarification about the kind of experience I want to analyze before I proceed. Perhaps no human activity is as over determined as sex. As feminists have variously demonstrated, sex is frequently the forum where a society plays out its most fundamental issues of power. Thus, the sounds of sex are all-too-often sounds of struggle, humiliation, and pain. When these sounds are overheard, they make for a very different experience than the aesthetic one I want to analyze. Sounds of forced pain, for example, make ethical demands on the hearer that undermine the distance necessary for aesthetic contemplation. It is for this reason that I focus on sounds marked primarily by their pleasure. I realize of course, that pain and pleasure are not necessarily bipolar opposites. Pain, especially in a sexual context, can be experienced as pleasurable, and pleasures are often complex and interlaced with aspects of pain. It still seems to me, however, that sounds can, with a fair amount of accuracy, be identified as pleasurable or painful, and it is the sounds of sexual pleasure that I want to interpret.

SEXUAL SOUNDS AS PRIMORDIAL TRUTH

The founding texts of modern philosophy are mostly epistemological, and the questions of whether we know anything at all about reality and what that might be are at the heart of what philosophy has been since Descartes. Some of the most important intellectual works of the last two hundred

---

3. Freud, "Dream and the Primal Scene," 29.
4. See Freud, *Three Essays on the Theory of Sexuality*.

Section I—Passionate Moments

years have been exposés of human claims to truth and objectivity. Marx, Nietzsche, and Foucault have shown the extent to which our deepest values are mired in ideologies of power; Freud has shown the many subtle ways our personal vision is determined by the vicissitudes of family history; and Wittgenstein has shown how the crucial epistemological tool of language is forged in, and contingent on, social forms of life. It would, though, be a mistake to confine this uncertainty about knowledge to the rarified air of philosophy. As Stanley Cavell has argued variously throughout his work, skeptical anxiety is critical to understanding some of the most influential texts and products of modernity, from *Hamlet* to the invention of photography. In other words, philosophers are not the only ones who seem caught in a web of subjectivity and metaphysical isolation. Modern individuality itself is virtually defined by its yearning for some translucent immediacy that might bypass the biases of its constructed nature and connect directly with reality.

Foucault's *History of Sexuality* is particularly revealing when read in the context of modernity's skeptical anxiety. As he analyzes "the discourses on sex in modern societies since the seventeenth century,"[5] he finds an obsession, not so much with sex itself as with the "truth of sex," sex as a guide to hidden metaphysical realities.

> Among its many emblems, our society wears that of the talking sex. The sex which one catches unawares and questions, and which, restrained and loquacious at the same time, endlessly replies . . . For many years, we have all been living in the realm of Prince Mangogul;[6] under the spell of an immense curiosity about sex, bent on questioning it, with an insatiable desire to hear it speak. . . . As if it were essential for us to be able to draw from that little piece of ourselves not only pleasure, a pleasure that comes of knowing pleasure, a knowledge-pleasure; and as if that fantastic animal we accommodate had itself such finely tuned ears, such searching eyes, so gifted a tongue and mind, as to know much and be quite willing to tell it[7].

Foucault is surely right about the proliferation of talk about sex, about our insatiable need to tell it and hear it told. The sheer volume and variety of

---

5. Foucault, *History of Sexuality*, 121.

6. A character in Diderot's fable "The Indiscreet Jewels" who acquires a magic ring, which will make women speak truthfully about their sexual activities and feelings.

7. Foucault, *History of Sexuality*, 77.

present-day talk about sex is astounding. And this talk is no longer relegated to dark corners; it is the staple of media talk shows, and a major subject even for mainstream press.

But, more importantly, I think Foucault is also right about the heavy metaphysical weight we have asked sex to carry, as if all of modernity's epistemological fears are trained on it, as if libido were more fundamental than any *cogito*, as if sex holds the key to our skeptical predicament. In other words, our modern obsession with sex is understandable only in the context of our modern obsession with truth.

It is amidst such yearning and anxieties that the modern person overhears the sounds of sexual pleasure. They seem to be immediate and direct, an involuntary noise that the body makes when stimulated in a certain way. They seem to possess an automaticity similar to a dog's yelp of pain. Just as it would be misleading to see the dog's yelp as a "sign" of pain, that is, as a unit unto itself capable of acquiring its own subjective meanings, so too seem the sounds of pleasure. There is an aura of primordiality surrounding them, as if they have their origins in an immediacy prior to the social constructions of language. The word "*plaisir*" might be claimed to have a French style, and the word "pleasure" an English style, but sexual moaning seems to sound across cultures and be, as it were, in pleasure's own style.

Granted, language is often present in the intensifying sounds of sex, but it is usually in the form of single words or short phrases, which only serves to deepen this aura of primordiality. Expletives are frequent, as are sacred or sacrilegious words. The cadence and rhythm of such words, however, are not those of normal speech, but closer to bodily sounds. It is almost as if these words are themselves on the border between grunt and speech, re-enacting a primal scene of our species' verbal beginnings.

One final quality of sexual sounds that re-enforces the "aura of origins" that they create is their ambiguity. Freud noted that children who witness sex, either visually or aurally, often mistake it for violence. Even to the experienced ear, moans of pleasure and pain can, at first, be indistinguishable, the strenuous breathing of sex be mistaken for that of other tasks. It is almost as if these sounds originate from a primordial time when the sensations were blurred and distinctions not yet fully evolved.

Taken together, these aspects of sexual sounds assure that when they are overheard in circumstances that allow for some measure of contemplation they will take on the power of the primordial and convey an "aura of origins." Captivated by this aura, the hearer delights in such a rare

Section I—Passionate Moments

metaphysical occurrence: the unmediated expression of pleasure itself, a perfectly translucent representation.

SEXUAL SOUNDS AS CONVENTIONALLY CONSTRUCTED

Yet, if we are taking Paul Simon's Lincoln Duncan as a guide, his wry detachment seems a far cry from the excitement of someone privy to metaphysical origins. This is because, I would argue, such excitement marks only the beginning of the overhearing experience, its "first movement," as it were. Since Duncan has been hearing the sounds all night long, they take on a quite different meaning to his sleepy ears. This change in meaning is a virtually inevitable "second movement" whenever the sounds persist over any length of time or are repeated several times in a series.

To Duncan's jaded ear, the sounds have come to lose any natural immediacy they were once thought to possess. In fact, they now seem to him like entries in some kind of contest. Although this contest is obviously an unofficial one, its rules can be quite rigid and far-reaching. To use Foucault again, it is a contest constructed by the omnipresent discourse of sexuality. This discourse determines not just how we talk about sex, but how we imagine it, and even how we perform the sound of it.

In our society, for example, an adolescent experiences thousands of media kisses before she engages in one herself. These images establish a certain norm for every aspect of this action, from its heterosexuality to its appropriate sounds. An unconscious standard becomes embedded into the bodily activity itself. The contest then, in which every member of society is an inescapable participant, involves measuring up to that standard. What Foucault calls a "normalizing gaze"[8] is internalized in every psyche, and exerts an unrelenting pressure, a form of performance anxiety.

Although the mechanics of my example are oversimplified, the underlying point is, I hope, clear. Even with something as biological as sexual activity, we do not just instinctively "do it"; we have to learn what "doing it" means. Thus, not only the patterns of our courtship, but even the modulated tones of our pleasure are products of cultural construction.

In younger days, I spent my first night in Paris in a European style hotel whose rooms opened onto a small courtyard. It was a sultry August night, and through the unairconditioned window I heard the unmistakable rhythm of sexual sounds. I drifted off into a jet-lagged sleep, elated by how

---

8. Foucault, *Discipline and Punish*, 184.

perfectly Parisian such a night lullaby seemed to be. It did not dawn on me until some nights later, while I was exploring the liberated possibilities of late night French television, that my perfect Parisian lullaby was most likely a soft core program playing a bit too loudly.

But my disappointment upon realizing that the sounds I overheard were really coming from a television set would be misunderstood if it seemed to validate a distinction between real sexual sounds and feigned ones, as if my experience would have been "real" had I overheard actual persons in the midst of sexual activity. My disappointment ended up running much deeper than that.

There is a frequently replayed scene from Rob Reiner's romantic comedy, *When Harry Met Sally* (1989),[9] where Harry (Billy Crystal) boasts to his friend Sally (Meg Ryan) over lunch that he can tell whenever a woman is faking an orgasm. Casually, Sally proceeds to "fake" an orgasm, causing quite a stir among the other restaurant patrons overhearing her sexual sounds.

The problem this scene raises for me is not the standard skeptical problem of other minds; whether one can ever know if another person is really in pleasure. In that problem, the issue is how to tell the difference between sounds that are genuinely felt and simulated ones. My problem, however, is whether there is really any difference to tell.

Noting that Meg Ryan's climax falls into the same rhythmically cadenced "yes" as Molly Bloom's famous climax at the end of *Ulysses* is not so much to unmask plagiarism as to recognize its impossibility. Jean Baudrillard has written perceptively about this situation in contemporary culture, a situation he calls the "precession of simulacra."[10] He uses the example of "holdups" (armed robberies) to explain this concept. Even if one supposes that there was a time when movies simulated actual robberies, now the direction is usually reversed. The weapons used, the masks worn, the commands issued appear first in the media. Baudrillard claims that the situation today has become so convoluted that a distinction between the original and the simulated is no longer tenable. "Of the same order as the impossibility of rediscovering an absolute level of the real, is the impossibility of staging an illusion. Illusion is no longer possible, because the real is no longer possible."[11]

9. Reiner, *When Harry Met Sally.*
10. Baudrillard, *Simulations*, 1.
11. Baudrillard, *Simulations*, 38.

Section I—Passionate Moments

The validity of Baudrillard's description affects the overhearing of sexual sounds. Although the experience begins with hopes for revelations of metaphysical secrets, those hopes evaporate rather quickly once the sounds extend over any length of time. For all the fervor of the sexual musicians, the hearer cannot but be struck by the conventionality of the music. Rather than echoing primordial mysteries, they end up echoing only current fashion. This process often moves the hearer beyond mere disappointment and into cynicism.

SEXUAL SOUNDS AS AESTHETIC PLAY

Although Duncan is on the verge of such a cynicism, he does not succumb. Since he has been hearing the sounds all night long, he is certainly not caught up in any metaphysical awe over them. But also, even though he acknowledges the inevitable artificiality of the sounds, he does not seem adrift or trapped, like Baudrillard, inside an endless precession of simulacra. Rather, the sounds become for him a musical beginning because they awaken memories and move him to create the song of his own story.

His story literally begins, of course, amidst the sexual sounds of his own conception: the music made by his fishing village mother and father. And even though there is no special revelatory power in these sounds, even though they are an indistinguishable combination of primal instincts, cultural fashion, and personal dreams, they are still the music played at every begetting, and Duncan is right to connect them with his own origins. Likewise, there is also something inevitable and fitting about connecting the sounds he is overhearing to his own history of sexual pleasure, as if to sing one's own song is to situate it amidst the vast cacophony of sexual sounds emitted from the planet.

As the sexual sounds drew Duncan to his own biological beginnings and his own sexual awakening, so too do they draw any listener fortunate enough to overhear them. They are, for the listener, a rudimentary theater of origins, and the origin being played out in this theater transcends the merely personal. Humans do not just live their pleasures and pains, they symbolize them; or, to put it more exactly, they live only symbolized pleasures and pains. No one says this better, I think, than Wallace Stevens in his poem "Men Made Out of Words"

> What should we be without the sexual myth,
> The human reverie or poem of death?
> Castratos of moon-mash—Life consists
> Of propositions about life. [12]

If sexual sounds, aesthetically contemplated, are about our origins as symbolizers, it is not surprising that they dramatize the dialectal poles of how we think about symbols. As I have traced the overhearing of these sounds, it begins with some muddled version of a correspondence theory: that the entire complexity of any symbolic system is anchored by an isomorphic fit between symbol and object in the world. This gives way to realization that there is something utterly arbitrary about symbols, and that an infinity of symbolic systems is possible, no one more anchored than any other.

As I have shown, this second movement has a down side. The promises that the sounds of sex offered when first overheard, promises of ready access to our origins, of pure and perfect expression of feeling, now come up empty. The utterly conventional, arbitrary character of symbols reveals reality to be inherently beyond us. This hard truth tempts us toward self-pity, toward a cynicism that sees no sound as more valuable than any other, no song as really worth singing.

But, while cynical despair is a common enough option, it is not, Derrida reminds us, the only one. The loss of an anchor definitely can leave one feeling alienated and adrift, but it can also leave one exhilarated with new-found freedom: the infinite freedom of symbolization. It is to this freedom, to this "joyous affirmation of the free play of the world and without truth, without origin, offered to our active interpretation,"[13] that Derrida calls us.

It is precisely this Derridean spirit of "freeplay" that seems closest to where Duncan is at the end of his song, and it also seems to me to best characterize the aesthetic delight taken in overhearing the strange symbolization that is the sound of sex. What amazes Duncan most, both on the night of his own first sexual sounds and on this night of overhearing others in the next room, are his fingers. His amazement at them, his gratitude for them, seems to be caused not so much by the delicacies they have touched, as by the sounds that the touching creates, sounds that include the dance of his fingers into the notes he is playing. Something like this amazement, this gratitude for the act of symbolization itself, explains the unique delight

---

12. Stevens, *Palm at the End of the Mind*, 281.
13. Derrida, "Structure, Sign and Play," 240.

Section I—Passionate Moments

of the person overhearing, contemplating, enjoying sexual sounds. Perhaps nowhere else could the infinite play of signification be so clearly dramatized and quite so beautiful.

BIBLIOGRAPHY

Baudrillard, Jean. *Simulations*. Translated by Paul Foss, Paul Patton, and Philip Beitchman. New York: Semiotext(e), 1983.
Cavell, Stanley. *The Cavell Reader*. Edited by Stephen Mulhall. Cambridge, MA: Blackwell, 1996.
———. *The Claim of Reason*. Oxford: Oxford University Press, 1979.
Derrida, Jacques. "Structure, Sign and Play in the Discourse of the Human Sciences." In *A Postmodern Reader*, edited by Joseph Natoli and Linda Hutcheon. New York: State University of New York Press, 1993.
Foucault, Michel. *Discipline and Punish*. Translated by Alan Sheridan. New York: Vintage, 1979.
———. *The History of Sexuality, Volume I: An Introduction*. Translated by Robert Hurley. New York: Vintage, 1990.
———. *Power/Knowledge*. Translated by Colin Gordon. New York: Pantheon, 1977.
Freud, Sigmund. "The Dream and the Primal Scene." In *The Standard Edition of the Complete Psychological Works of Sigmund Freud*, edited by James Strachey, 29–47. Translated by James Strachey. London: Hogarth Press, 1955.
———. *Introductory Lectures on Psychoanalysis*. Translated and edited by James Strachey. New York: W. W. Norton, 1966.
———. *Three Essays on the Theory of Sexuality*. Edited by James Strachey. New York: Avon, 1962.
Joyce, James. *Ulysses*. New York: Modern Library, 1914.
Marx, Karl. *The Essential Writings*. Edited by Frederic L. Bender. Boulder, CO: Westview, 1972.
Nietzsche, Friedrich. *The Will to Power*. Translated by Walter Kaufmann and R.J. Hollingdale. New York: Vintage, 1967.
Reiner, Rob, dir. *When Harry Met Sally*. US; 1989; Castle Rock Entertainment. Distributed by Columbia Pictures.
Simon, Paul. *The Songs of Paul Simon*. New York: Alfred A. Knopf, 1974.
Stevens, Wallace. *The Palm at the End of the Mind*. Edited by Holly Stevens. New York: Macmillan, 1972.
Wittgenstein, Ludwig. *Philosophical Investigations*. Translated by G.E.M. Anscombe. New York: Macmillan, 1958.

Pornophony

Maggie Ann Labinski

INTRODUCTION

In "An Aesthetic Reading of Sexual Sounds," James Conlon argues that contemplating the sounds of sexual pleasure is, itself, a source of delight. A key step towards accessing this "joy" is recognizing that these symbols are culturally conditioned.[1] We may initially believe that such moans and groans are spontaneous—that they offer "immediate and direct" access to "reality."[2] However, further examination reveals that they are simply the results of lessons already learned. Conlon explains:

> In our society, for example, an adolescent experiences thousands of media kisses before she engages in one herself. These images establish a certain norm for every aspect of this action, from its heterosexuality to its appropriate sounds ... Even with something as biological as sexual activity, we do not just instinctively "do it"; we have to learn what "doing it" means. Thus not only the patterns of our courtship, but even the modulated tones of our pleasure are products of cultural construction.[3]

Conlon admits that increasing our awareness of the conventionality of sexual sounds can foster "cynicism."[4] If we expect sex to open "primordial truths,"[5] if we believe such symbols connect us to something bigger than

---

1. Conlon, "Aesthetic Reading of Sexual Sounds," 58.
2. Conlon, "Aesthetic Reading of Sexual Sounds," 54.
3. Conlon, "Aesthetic Reading of Sexual Sounds," 56.
4. Conlon, "Aesthetic Reading of Sexual Sounds," 57.
5. Conlon, "Aesthetic Reading of Sexual Sounds," 53.

ourselves, it is easy to be frustrated by the knowledge that we have encountered these sounds before:

> The promises that the sounds of sex offered . . . promises of ready access to our origins, of pure and perfect expression of feeling, now come up empty. The utterly conventional, arbitrary character of symbols reveals reality to be inherently beyond us. This hard truth tempts us toward self-pity, toward a cynicism that sees no sound as more valuable than any other, no song as really worth singing.[6]

Nevertheless, Conlon concludes that there are more positive ways to interpret the state of our sexual affairs. Sex may be a sophisticated social construct, but this implies the presence of an equally sophisticated social constructor. Rather than grieving for a "metaphysical" opportunity that never was,[7] Conlon proposes that we embrace the "freedom" of our own aesthetic potential—our unique ability to create sounds, to "play" with sexual symbols:

> But while cynical despair is a common enough option, it is not, as Derrida reminds us, the only one. The loss of an anchor definitely can leave one feeling alienated and adrift, [but] it can also leave one exhilarated with a newfound freedom: the infinite freedom of symbolization . . . [the] "joyous affirmation of the freeplay of the world . . . offered to our active interpretation."[8]

It is this realization that grounds the unique pleasures of contemplation. There is delight to be had in the discovery that one has lost "an anchor." There is joy to be found in learning that we are able to manipulate sexual symbols as we will. So understood, Conlon not only redeems sex as an object worthy of rigorous analysis. He also highlights the "aesthetic" benefits of placing sex in the hands of contemplative disciplines like philosophy.

QUESTION

Conlon's insight has implications for all those who are exposed to the sounds of sexual pleasure. In addition, it would seem to raise important questions for those who teach courses on human sexuality—who formally

---

6. Conlon, "Aesthetic Reading of Sexual Sounds," 57.
7. Conlon, "Aesthetic Reading of Sexual Sounds," 57.
8. Conlon, "Aesthetic Reading of Sexual Sounds," 58.

encourage students to contemplate, to philosophize, about the ins and outs of sex. I am especially drawn to the optimism of his conclusion. I want it to be the case that the conventionality of sex might lead us to relish in the gift of human symbolization. I would prefer to live in a world where the knowledge of sexual normativity might inspire delight, instead of despair. Unfortunately, when it comes to conveying such sentiments to my students, I fear that I am failing miserably. After we discuss the effects of "thousands of media kisses," they do not seem "exhilarated with a newfound freedom." After we analyze the cultural construction of sex, they are not drawn to the pleasures of aesthetic "play." No, much to my dismay, I appear to be in the business of producing sexual "cynics." While my students are decidedly generous with me, they seem less convinced that philosophy is at all generous with sex. As one student put it recently: "Are we still supposed to *like* sex after learning all this stuff?"

I imagine that some measure of the trouble I have caused is due to my general tendency to emphasize the political to the detriment of the aesthetic.[9] The majority of my courses draw from feminist philosophies, and much of this scholarship has been pointed in its criticism of the broader systemic dangers of sex.[10] There is, arguably, little room for pleasure when one operates with an eye towards the pain of widespread sexual oppression. In this particular instance, I find myself immediately suspicious about the extent of our freedom to symbolize. It is the "infinite" freedom of such "play" that Conlon cites as the condition of our delight. It is the complete openness of sex to our aesthetic desires that he argues might woo even the "cynic." Somewhere along the way, I lost faith in this freedom. More specifically, I worry that our sexual sounds are at least partially limited insofar as they remain caught within the political abuses of our symbolic traditions.

The existence of these abuses has been well documented. For example, as Conlon intimates, the "play" of symbols in the West has a long history of serving to normalize white heterosexuality.[11] This manipulation of sexual privilege is often accomplished through our encounters with "thousands of media kisses." Such cultural exchanges not only teach us how to make sounds. They teach us how to use them. We are taught to wield symbols to

---

9. I do not mean to suggest that the boundaries between art and politics are clear-cut. Art is political, and at least some philosophers have maintained that (properly ordered) politics can be beautiful.

10. See Mackinnon, "Feminism, Marxism, Method," and Dworkin, *Intercourse*.

11. Conlon, "Aesthetic Reading of Sexual Sounds," 56.

affirm some lives and deny others. As Adrienne Rich argues, this political lesson—this either/or approach to human sexuality—has been one of the most recurring themes throughout the Western construction of sex:

> We have been stalled in a maze of false dichotomies which prevents our apprehending the institution as a whole: 'good' versus 'bad' marriages, 'marriage for love' versus arranged marriage; 'liberated' sex versus prostitution; heterosexual intercourse versus rape ... Within the institution exist qualitative differences of experience; but the absence of choice remains the great unacknowledged reality.[12]

While the popularity of certain sexual practices, the appeal of select sounds, comes and goes, the use of sex to draw lines across our communities has stayed more or less the same.

The hope, of course, is that we can unlearn these lessons. The hope is that the political challenge of deconstructing sexual privilege is comparable to the aesthetic challenge of adding more beautiful sounds to our repertoires. My concern is that, even if this hope can be realized, the effects of these traditions linger—effects that inevitably curtail the scope of our "play." Perhaps the strongest evidence of this lingering is the fact that the manipulation of our freedom to symbolize continues. Even today, the media-majority in the West largely refuses to humor the possibility that sex should bring us together, rather than drive us apart. The transmission of this ideology is especially pronounced in the sexual messages targeted to children.[13] A quick glance at the top rated films from Disney and Pixar confirms that we are a long way from emboldening our young girls to dream of the day when "their princess will come." Certain kisses are still considered off limits. Certain sounds fall outside the "thousands" that are reinforced. To follow Nina Hartley, when we silence such "dreams" we silence the range of our sexual voices.[14] We make the creative journey towards some sounds more arduous, if not altogether impossible. Our freedom to "play" is, in other words, shaped by the contours of the game we have been given—a game produced by the brandishing of political power as much as any individual aesthetic choice.

---

12. Rich, *Compulsory Heterosexuality and Lesbian Existence*, 75.

13. For an account of one of the many consequences of these sexual messages, see Bishop, "The Making of a Pre-Pubescent Porn Star."

14. Hartley, *Porn*, 234.

So, too, one might consider the growing list of sexual symbols that would seem to have been irrevocably broken by this politics of division. For instance, many feminists have argued that the sounds at work in the ritual of marriage have been tied to these abuses for so long that they can no longer be retrieved.[15] As Claudia Card maintains, there are consequences to history.[16] Regardless as to how counter-cultural we may intend the sounds of our own 'I do's,' they still share the same patriarchal beginning. They still ride on the backs of centuries of women who were exchanged as pieces of sexual property. While we may be free to ignore the cries of these women, while we may be free to be outraged by their mistreatment, it is less clear that we are free to deny their place in our symbolic consciousness.[17] It is less clear that we are free to claim that the sounds of our "first kisses" have a meaning that is radically independent from their pain.

Finally, one might take into account the figure Conlon offers as the exemplar of contemplative pleasure—i.e., Lincoln Duncan from Paul Simon's song of the same name.[18] Conlon suggests that, upon hearing the sounds of a couple having sex through his motel wall, Duncan begins to weave the symbols of his sexual past with the present. At each moment, Conlon proposes, Duncan's posture is defined by "gratitude:"

> What amazes Duncan most, both on the night of his own first sexual sounds and on this night of overhearing others in the next room, are his fingers. His amazement at them, his gratitude for them, seems to be caused not so much by the delicacies they have touched, as by the sounds that the touching creates, sounds that include the dance of his fingers into the notes he is playing. Something like this amazement, this gratitude for the act of symbolization itself, explains the unique delight of the person overhearing, contemplating, enjoying sexual sounds.[19]

Unfortunately, the delight that Duncan discovers—"the notes he is playing"—would also seem to be very much in keeping with certain traditional political hierarchies. These include the assumed centrality of his own male

---

15. See Firestone, *Dialectic of Sex*; Jeffreys, "Need to Abolish Marriage;" Millett, *Sexual Politics*.

16. Card, "Against Marriage and Motherhood."

17. For a less sexually oriented analysis of the effects of this kind of consciousness, see Cabreros-Sud, "Kicking Ass."

18. Conlon, "Aesthetic Reading of Sexual Sounds," 51.

19. Conlon, "Aesthetic Reading of Sexual Sounds," 58.

Section I—Passionate Moments

perspective. As Elizabeth Spelman argues, the Western canon is largely characterized by the dominance of male voices and the systematic exclusion of women, especially women of color.[20] The denial of these insights perpetuates the notion that women are secondary—a footnote to 'legitimate' human experience. This includes the experience of human sexuality. One can see such denial reinforced in Duncan's contemplative "amazement." For example, the young woman whom Duncan identifies as most instrumental in shaping his use of symbols, in producing his pleasure, is never named. Like many women in Western history, she remains unknown and nearly voiceless. Furthermore, Duncan mentions nothing about *her* sounds—her delight. While Duncan is certainly aware that there are other symbolizers in the world,[21] this awareness does not lead him to act as if her "play" is worthy of his consideration. My point is not that Duncan (or Paul Simon) willfully intended to dismiss this experience. My point is only that, here too, the political context within which Duncan finds pleasure narrows the otherwise "infinite" potential of his music. Duncan is free to take joy in ways that deny this woman a name. But, he is not free to assert that this joy unfolds in a symbolic world where denial has served women well.

These are the sorts of issues that have diminished my hope and dominated my syllabi. Given their severity, my student's question is not surprising. How could I expect them to "still like sex" after fifteen weeks of toiling through "all this [political] stuff?" How could I have convinced myself that they would find pleasure in the contemplation of sex when I gave them no reason to believe that there is anything this process might provide to feel optimistic about? In all fairness, I am not entirely prepared to ignore "political stuff" altogether. I would be remiss if students left my classes without some exposure to the tragedies of the West and the ways these events encroach upon their sexual choices. Still, I *am* drawn to Conlon's optimism. I do agree that my students deserve to investigate the possibility that the contemplation of sex can also lead to joy—that sexual acts "move us by the meaning and intensity of their beauty."[22]

Given this, I wonder about the pedagogical benefits of working towards a kind of both/and—i.e., of allowing the beauty of Conlon's aesthetics to stand alongside the political ugliness of our traditions. Is it possible to

---

20. Spelman argues that this process of exclusion can be seen within feminist philosophies as well. See Spelman, *Inessential Woman*.

21. Conlon, "Aesthetic Reading of Sexual Sounds," 55.

22. Conlon, "Aesthetic Reading of Sexual Sounds," 52.

cultivate pleasure around the analysis of symbolic practices that are decidedly less free—that are tempered by the past, though eager for the future? Might the process of contemplation help us to take delight in our aesthetic abilities, without ignoring the restraints put in place by an ongoing history of sexual injustice? More pressingly, I wonder if there are concrete examples of sexual sounds that I could offer my students to encourage such thinking—symbols whose study might present a viable alternative to either unfettered "gratitude" or unnecessary "cynicism?"

THE SOUNDS OF FEMINIST PORN

To this end, I would like to argue that one example can be found in the sounds of feminist porn.[23] The precise boundaries of feminist porn remain open to debate.[24] Still, there are some traits that the bulk of this industry shares in common. Most notably, one of the central goals of feminist porn has been to call into question those problematic symbolic traditions that impose themselves upon our sexual communities. In contrast to the types of media produced by the mainstream industry, feminist pornographers have sought to create porn that challenges institutional sexism, racism, homophobia, etc. At its most basic level, feminist porn uses sex to reclaim sex. By creatively retrieving the whats and hows of sexual activity on set, these films encourage the creative retrieval of sex in 'the city.' The editors of *The Feminist Porn Book* explain:

> [F]eminist porn uses sexually explicit imagery to contrast and complicate dominant representations of gender, sexuality, race, ethnicity, class, ability, age, body type, and other identity markers. It explores concepts of desire, agency, power, beauty, and pleasure at their most confounding and difficult . . . It seeks to unsettle conventional definitions of sex, and expand the language of sex . . . Feminist porn creates alternative images and develops its own aesthetics and iconography to expand established sexual norms and discourses.[25]

---

23. The symbols that comprise feminist porn are not limited to audible sounds. However, given that this is Conlon's focus, I will follow suit.

24. Few topics have divided feminists as much as that of pornography. For an overview of both sides of the "sex wars" see Cornel, *Feminism and Pornography*.

25. Taormino et al., "Introduction," 9–10.

Section I—Passionate Moments

To help achieve this goal—to better "complicate," "unsettle," and "expand" sex—feminist porn has focused on those voices that have, thus far, been silenced by the effects of "thousands of media kisses." In particular, feminist porn has sought to make a space for the pleasures of women.[26] The desire to capture and reproduce such under-represented delights has led these films to embody two distinct positions on sex and sexuality.

On the one hand, the sounds of feminist porn operate in full support of aesthetic "play." The working assumption behind this industry is that sex is open to our transformation. What are we to do when the erotic symbols we are given deny the perspectives of most human beings? How are we to respond to a tradition of sexual mis-education? We create new symbols. We develop different sounds. We make sex 'better.' We make 'better' porn. For example, as Tristan Taormino remarks, many of the earliest pieces of feminist porn sought to redefine popular conceptions of what "counts" as "doing it."[27]

> Feminist porn . . . is committed to depicting diversity in gender, race, ethnicity, nationality, sexuality, class, body size, ability, and age. Feminist porn also challenges what constitutes sex itself and the heteronormative depictions of penis-in-vagina (or ass) intercourse as the ultimate, climactic act and everything else as some sort of inconsequential window dressing.[28]

Instead of reducing the joys of sex to the moment of white male orgasm, directors here explored sexual acts that had previously been labeled as either foreplay or perversion.[29] As a result, these films captured sounds that had not existed within mainstream pornography. After all, they had not "counted" as being the sounds of "legitimate" sexual pleasure.[30]

Such symbolic innovation has served as a source of aesthetic inspiration for feminist pornographers and the feminist community writ large. The "play" surrounding the symbolization of sexual consent is a valuable case in point. A number of feminists have argued that one of the most serious problems with traditional pornography is the absence of the sound of

---

26. For example, Candida Royalle argues for the importance of "a female vision or point of view." See Royalle, "What's a Nice Girl Like You . . . ," 62.

27. This question can be seen in feminist philosophies of sex and sexuality in general. See Christina, "Are We Having Sex Now or What," 3–8.

28. Taormino, "Calling the Shots," 262.

29. See also Lee, "Uncategorized."

30. Gayle Rubin uses the language of the "charmed circle." See Rubin, "Thinking Sex."

radical consent.[31] This silence infers that consent falls outside the boundaries of the activity of sex proper. It suggests that consent is, at best, an annoying preamble—an exchange that occurs before anything 'worthwhile' happens. By extension, the lack of these sounds insinuates that the symbolization of consent is fundamentally un-pleasurable. Pornography is in the business of marketing pleasure, and anything less will be left on the editing floor. In contrast to this position, feminist porn has striven to re-eroticize the vocalization of consent.[32] As Lorelei Lee intimates, these sounds begin with open and honest dialogue on set:

> This is when working in pornography truly became exciting to me . . . [I]t was on set that I was first asked this powerful question: What do you want to do? There is a kind of irony in the fact that people so often link pornography with coercion, when it is on porn sets that I really learned what it is to give consent. Never in a civilian sexual encounter had I been explicitly asked what I was and wasn't willing to do with my body.[33]

The sharing of sexual consent can be a highly "exciting" moment, indeed. Regrettably, far too many "civilian sexual encounters" take the Sleeping Beauty narrative as their guide—demoting an explicit 'yes' to the terms of half-conscious innuendo. By highlighting the delights possible in these symbols, feminist porn invites all of us to reconsider the pleasures of this "play," the joys of sexual agency and empowerment.

At the same time, and on the other hand, feminist porn has, almost without exception, been adamant about the limits of their symbolic achievements. As Mireille Miller-Young explains, though motivated by a different politics, feminist porn does not purport to exist in a different political world:

> Though feminism seeks to dismantle structural and discursive exploitation and oppression of women and marginalized populations, our feminist praxis is not external to or untouched by [these] systems of domination. Theorizing a feminist pornography then means thinking about a dual process of transgression and restriction.[34]

31. See Dworkin, *Pornography*.

32. As Rachel Kramer Bussel argues, this need not entail the commodification of consent. See Bussel, "Beyond Yes or No," 48.

33. Lee, "Cum Guzzling Anal Nurse Whore," 209.

34. Miller-Young, Interventions, 107.

Section I—Passionate Moments

There is delight to be found in the "play" of symbols. There is joy to be had in sounds that seek to change the sexual landscape. But, such production and reproduction occurs against a tarnished political backdrop. This backdrop has often resulted in the inadvertent upholding of problematic sexual norms. Feminist porn has, despite itself, composed symphonies that have reinforced the very traditions it longs to change.

Such inadequacies are evident in the complex relationship between feminist porn and the sounds of "hard core" sex.[35] The pioneers of feminist porn generally avoided "hard core" scenes, claiming that these acts were targeted exclusively to a male audience. Given the desire to tend to the pleasures of women, feminist directors sought to create media with a "softer" aesthetic. Through the work of individuals like Candida Royalle, feminist porn became synonymous with the "play" of a specific set of symbols—i.e., symbols that presented sex as "gentler, more romantic."[36] The intentions of such directors were, arguably, progressive. Regrettably, much of the porn they produced "played" right into the hand of the sexual narratives they opposed. For example, many have argued that some of these films perpetuated dangerous myths about gender, including that of the binary gender system itself. As Jane Ward suggests, the theory that "women" prefer "softer" sex raises more questions than answers. Who do we mean by "women?" Where do "women's" desires come from? And, who benefits from the association between "the feminine" and the pleasures of sexual "softness?" Ward states:

> [These] approaches to sexuality privilege women's genuine desires and experiences, but it does so without much critical reflection on who we think women are, and how they come to desire what they do . . . Sure, market research may indicate that women do, in fact, have group preferences (for deeper plot narratives, close-ups of female orgasms, and so on), but even these "feminist" preferences have been marketed to us, and arguably mirror simplistic cultural constructions of femininity.[37]

Part of what has made feminist porn unique is that such concerns, the present case included, often originate from within. Few are as critical of the political shortcomings of feminist porn than the creators of this genre themselves. More importantly, the recognition of their own limits has only fueled the aesthetic flame, incited the desire to "play." This industry remains

---

35. See Williams, *Hard Core*.
36. Taormino et al., "Introduction," 11.
37. Ward, "Queer Feminist Pigs," 135.

in motion—expanding and contracting so that its symbols might better address the realities of a changing world. Early innovators like Candida Royalle continue to return to the drawing board, prepared to "play" until feminist porn has achieved all it set out to accomplish.[38] While this development does not change the fact that the pleasures one hears in feminist porn can fall flat, it does convey the message that sexual symbolization is never complete. Our aesthetic potential is, surely, a gift. It is also a responsibility—one as necessary as the feminist movement/s today.

In sum, the sounds of feminist porn reflect a complex stance on a complex issue. The symbols that one might encounter in these films encourage the acknowledgement of both our aesthetic abilities and the political frameworks that bear upon them. Feminist pornographers offer a compelling model of what it means to delight in the possibilities of sexual symbols, all the while knowing that there is more to be done before these symbols are able to express everything we might long for. By extension, the contemplation of such sounds opens (what I would call) a kind of critical-pleasure. To analyze the "play" of feminist porn is to admit that our sounds are not as "free" as we may hope. However, the only option is to keep "playing"—to rework our symbols until they match our political aspirations. It is the pleasure of *this* understanding that I think might benefit my students and address the gaps in my pedagogy. One may rightly experience joy when faced with the knowledge of their own infinite potential. But, there is also delight to be uncovered in finitude—in the recognition that our flawed steps are still a part of the process, that moving sideways is better than not moving at all, that melodies sung off-key are often but one note away from harmony. Of course, thinking about such "play" in the classroom is far from un-contentious. Exploring porn with others rarely is. Nevertheless, it does seem that there are advantages to investigating these films with students. More specifically, if our students can find pleasure in the activity of contemplation they may well keep doing it. Our shared sexual future depends upon students leaving our classes eager to continue the journey—excited to participate in the simultaneously aesthetic and political task of "complicating," "unsettling," and "expanding" sex.

---

38. See Royalle's reconsideration of porn with a "raw edge." Royalle, "Porn in the USA," 28–29.

Section I—Passionate Moments

THE SOUNDS OF PEDAGOGICAL PLEASURE

My partner is also an academic, and I often have him read my work before I force it onto others. When he finished reading this, his response was more negative than usual. "You just can't," he said, shaking his head. "Your teacher is going to hate this." I was prepared for him to point to some issue in my logic or source material, which he is (almost annoyingly) good at doing. Yet, his problem rested elsewhere. "Your teacher is going to hate it," he said. "I don't care how 'postmodern' this guy is; no one wants a student to use their work to justify showing porn in class."

Perhaps he is right. There is a lot here that suggests that this apple fell very far from her tree. At a minimum, it is unlikely that the sounds of feminist porn even fall within the set of sexual symbols that Conlon would have us consider. Near the beginning of his article, Conlon makes a list of caveats that clarify the parameters of his analysis. One of these concerns the difference between what he calls the sounds of "real life" and those that are "performed:"

> My analytic interest here is . . . that area called the aesthetics of everyday life. In other words, the sexual sounds I am concerned with originate in the context of a real life intimacy assumed by the participants to be private; if the sounds are consciously performed before an audience, they lose a crucial part of their meaning.[39]

It is uncertain if the "public" sounds of porn carry the same weight as the "private" sounds that occur in our bedrooms. It is unclear if the kind of symbolization we encounter in porn overlaps in a meaningful way with the pleasures of "real life." One wonders if these sounds are even deserving of contemplation, of philosophy. Would our students not be better served elsewhere?

I am happy to grant that there are differences between sexual sounds. So, too, I share Conlon's misgivings about those symbols that lack any connection to authentic human "intimacy." However, I do not know if we must concede that the sounds of pleasure we "consciously perform"—like the sounds of pornography—are totally separate from the pleasures of "real life." I am reluctant to claim that such melodies lack "meaning" simply because they are produced "before an audience." Ironically enough, I attribute this sentiment, this optimism, to my teacher as well. To better explain, and

---

39. Conlon, "Aesthetic Reading of Sexual Sounds," 52.

to conclude, I want to briefly call to mind a final site of Conlon's influence over me—not as it pertains to the sounds of sex, but the sounds of education.

One of the first things that bemused me when I started teaching was how much of *it* is a performance. I am reminded of this every time I teach back-to-back sections of the same course and realize that I have told the same joke, at the same moment, multiple times, in the same afternoon. Some scholars have criticized the notion of "performance pedagogy," suggesting that it reflects a top-down understanding of education that over-exaggerates the centrality of the teacher. Still, without denying these concerns, it seems one might reasonably argue that there are at least some aspects of teaching that cannot be entirely spontaneous. As Jyl Felman argues, it is up to teachers to use their "craft" wisely—to ensure that any pedagogical "routine" implicates themselves as well as their students:

> What makes this performance Feminist and not Patriarchal is the fact that I too am transformed, even while in the process of transforming. There is continuous reciprocity on this stage between actor and audience, teacher and student. For this is live performance at its most electrifying, where the denouement depends on the students themselves.[40]

While I was a student at Mount Mary, Conlon's courses always seemed to steal the show. His classroom was "live performance at its most electrifying." For me, what truly set his courses apart was less the grandeur of the routine. It was his willingness to incorporate his pleasure. We are taught that philosophy translates to the "love of wisdom." Yet, if I am honest, what I fell in love with so many years ago was not wisdom. I fell in love with the sounds of my teacher's delight. I fell in love with his willingness to give voice to his pleasure in front of us—to implicate himself in the performance of teaching. It is this risk of self-implication that, I would argue, ties a sound to "real life." It was the opportunity to participate in such "continuous reciprocity" that drew me to Conlon's classes over and over again. And, it is the embodiment of such vulnerability within our broken sexual world that I also hear in the performance of feminist porn.[41]

So, too, I think it is my hesitancy to implicate myself with my own students that has been missing in my classes. My student asked, "Are *we* still

---

40. Felman, *Never A Dull Moment*, xvii.

41. One can see in the autobiographical accounts of those who work in the industry. See Lee, *Coming Out Like a Porn Star*.

supposed to like sex after learning all this stuff." But, I think she meant, "Do *you*? Does sex still give *you* pleasure at the end of the day? Does contemplating it still leave *you* exhilarated?" Unlike my teacher, my pleasure has been hiding. And, it is only here, where the risk is less—where I am allowed to "play" the student—that I feel "free" enough to admit: "Yes, yes, yes!"[42] Sex inspires me, even after it has been put through the analytic ringer. And, teaching about it brings me pleasure as well. For I once heard the "real life" sounds of a philosopher's joy.

BIBLIOGRAPHY

Bishop, Marcia J. "The Making of a Pre-Pubescent Porn Star: Contemporary Fashion for Elementary School Girls." In *Pop Porn: Pornography in American Culture*, edited by Ann C. Hall and Mardia J. Bishop, 45–56. Westport, CT: Praeger, 2007.

Bussel, Rachel Kramer. "Beyond Yes or No: Consent as Sexual Process." In *Yes Means Yes: Visions of Female Sexual Power and a World Without Rape*, edited by Jaclyn Friedman and Jessica Valenti, 43–52. Berkeley: Seal, 2008.

Cabreros-Sud, Veena. "Kicking Ass." In *To Be Real: Telling the Truth and Changing the Face of Feminism*, edited by Rebecca Walker, 41–47. New York: Anchor, 1995.

Card, Claudia. "Against Marriage and Motherhood." *Hypatia* 11 (1996) 1–23.

Christina, Greta. "Are We Having Sex Now or What?" In *The Philosophy of Sex*, edited by Alan Soble, 3–8. Lanham, MD: Rowman & Littlefield, 2002.

Conlon, James. "An Aesthetic Reading of Sexual Sounds." *International Journal of Sexuality and Gender Studies* 7 (2002) 51–59.

Cornel, Drucilla, ed. *Feminism and Pornography*. Oxford: Oxford University Press, 2000.

Dworkin, Andrea. *Intercourse*. New York: Basic, 1987.

———. *Pornography: Men Possessing Women*. New York: Putnam, 1981.

Felman, Jyl Lynn. *Never a Dull Moment: Teaching and the Art of Performance*. New York: Routledge, 2001.

Firestone, Shulamith. *The Dialectic of Sex*. New York: Farrar, Straus, and Giroux, 1970.

Hartley, Nina. "Porn: An Effective Vehicle for Sexual Role Modeling and Education." In *The Feminist Porn Book*, edited by Tristan Taormino, Celine Parrenas Shimizu, Constance Penley, and Mireille Miller-Young, 228–36. New York: Feminist, 2013.

Jeffreys, Sheila. "The Need to Abolish Marriage." *Feminism and Psychology* 14 (2004) 327–31.

Lee, Jiz. "Uncategorized: Genderqueer Identity and Performance in Independent and Mainstream Porn." In *The Feminist Porn Book*, edited by Tristan Taormino, Celine Parrenas Shimizu, Constance Penley, and Mireille Miller-Young, 273–78. New York: Feminist, 2013.

Lee, Jiz, ed. *Coming Out Like a Porn Star: Essays on Pornography, Protection, and Privacy*. Berkeley: ThreeL Media, 2015.

---

42. Conlon, "Aesthetic Reading of Sexual Sounds," 56.

Lee, Lorelei. "Cum Guzzling Anal Nurse Whore: A Feminist Porn Star Manifesta." In *The Feminist Porn Book*, edited by Tristan Taormino, Celine Parrenas Shimizu, Constance Penley, and Mireille Miller-Young, 200–14. New York: Feminist, 2013.

Mackinnon, Catharine A. "Feminism, Marxism, Method, and the State: An Agenda for Theory." *Signs* 7 (1982) 515–44.

Miller-Young, Mireille. "Interventions: The Deviant and Defiant Art of Black Women Porn Directors." In *The Feminist Porn Book*, edited by Tristan Taormino, Celine Parrenas Shimizu, Constance Penley, and Mireille Miller-Young, 105–20. New York: Feminist, 2013.

Millett, Kate. *Sexual Politics*. New York: Columbia University Press, 1969.

Rich, Adrienne. "Compulsory Heterosexuality and Lesbian Existence." In *Blood, Bread, and Poetry*, 23–75. New York: W.W. Norton, 1986.

Royalle, Candida. "Porn in the USA." *Social Text* 37 (1993) 23–32.

———. "What's a Nice Girl Like You . . . " In *The Feminist Porn Book*, edited by Tristan Taormino, Celine Parrenas Shimizu, Constance Penley, and Mireille Miller-Young, 58–69. New York: Feminist, 2013.

Rubin, Gayle. "Thinking Sex: Notes for a Radical Theory of the Politics of Sexuality." In *Pleasure and Danger: Exploring Female Sexuality*, edited by Carole S. Vance, 267–319. Boston: Routledge & K. Paul, 1984.

Spelman, Elizabeth. *Inessential Woman*. Boston: Beacon Press, 1988.

Taormino, Tristan. "Calling the Shots: Feminist Porn in Theory and Practice." In *The Feminist Porn Book*, edited by Tristan Taormino, Celine Parrenas Shimizu, Constance Penley, and Mireille Miller-Young, 255–64. New York: Feminist, 2013.

Taormino, Tristan, et al. "Introduction: The Politics of Producing Pleasure." In *The Feminist Porn Book*, edited by Tristan Taormino, Celine Parrenas Shimizu, Constance Penley, and Mireille Miller-Young, 9–20. New York: Feminist, 2013.

Ward, Jane. "Queer Feminist Pigs: A Spectator's Manifesta." In *The Feminist Porn Book*, edited by Tristan Taormino, Celine Parrenas Shimizu, Constance Penley, and Mireille Miller-Young, 130–39. New York: Feminist, 2013.

Williams, Linda. *Hard Core: Power, Pleasure and the "Frenzy of the Visible."* Berkeley: University of California Press, 1989.

SECTION II

Transformative Moments
Teaching Philosophy's Relevance

Stanley Cavell and the Predicament of Philosophy[1]

JAMES CONLON

ONE WOULD LIKE TO think that the death of philosophy would cause some cultural concern; if not as much as that of god, at least as much as the death of the novel. But it would not. Perhaps that is why no one has bothered to proclaim it. Like no other area in the humanities, philosophy is isolated from the general culture and maintained by sheer academic will power. Its professionalism has made the work of its most respected practitioners accessible to only a few specialized colleagues. There are more scholarly articles than ever, but virtually no readers. Philosophy departments still attract graduate students, even talented ones, but their private talk reveals anxiety not just about whether philosophy can earn them a living, but whether it is a living at all. As if, like astrology or phrenology, it might continue to have its devotees, but cease to be an active participant in the conversation humanity has about itself. This is the predicament of philosophy.

In *Philosophy and the Mirror of Nature*, Richard Rorty argues that the intellectual giants philosophy spawned in this century, Dewey, Heidegger and Wittgenstein, all abandoned professional philosophy. They underwent a vocational crisis and moved on to other things, because they came to believe that doing philosophy simply wasn't contributing to human self-understanding.

Stanley Cavell is a professional philosopher who has undergone a similar crisis, but describes himself as "one who stayed."[2] Perhaps there

---

1. This paper was first published in the *Proceedings of the American Catholic Philosophical Association* 57 (1983) 88–97. It is reprinted in this volume with the permission of the ACPA.

2. Cavell, *Claim of Reason*, xviii.

Section II — Transformative Moments

would be protests that someone whose work consists of two books on film, a meditation on Thoreau, a collection of essays including "readings" of *Endgame* and *King Lear*, and a reworked dissertation, hardly qualifies as a professional philosopher. However, his work takes the form it does, precisely because of his honesty in facing the predicament of philosophy. As this paper will show, Cavell's work serves as an important gadfly to those who have claimed that role as their own.

To understand the predicament of philosophy in contemporary culture, one must start with understanding what philosophy is. But to ask that question is to ask what it does, how it functions. Meaning and use are inextricably intertwined. Thus, Cavell starts his own discussion of art in *The World Viewed* with a comparison between the kind of importance (use) art has and the kind of importance movies have.

> Music, painting, sculpture, poetry—as they are now sought by artists of major ambition, artists devoted to the making of objects meant as the live history of their art—are not generally important, except pretty much for the men and women devoted to creating them . . . . But rich and poor, those who care about no (other) art and those who live on the promise of art, those whose pride is education and those whose pride is power or practicality—all care about movies, await them, respond to them, remember them, talk about them, hate some of them, are grateful for some of them.[3]

I take this contrast between the importance of movies and the other arts to be obvious. And the importance is not simply that more people know John Wayne than know Picasso, but that Wayne means more to them, is a force affecting their own determination of meaning, in a way that Picasso simply isn't. Also, I take this unimportance to characterize the status of philosophy to a far greater degree than the arts. Few people could name a living philosopher, or even a philosophical work of this century. Philosophy is clearly not a factor which affects the ordinary achievements of human meaning.

Perhaps this is as it should be; perhaps this situation is the very nature of philosophy. But that would imply that philosophy has a self-understanding which explains why general importance is of no importance to it (as does nuclear physics, for example). Philosophy has no such explanation. It is increasingly insignificant to the culture and lacks any explanation (besides elitism) for why this insignificance is acceptable. This predicament is moving beyond the merely embarrassing to the scandalous.

3. Cavell, *World Viewed*, 41.

To explain how philosophy got into this predicament, Cavell suggests starting with the central characteristic of the modern age, its extreme self-consciousness, that is, modernism. "If it makes sense to speak of the Greeks as having discovered the self, or of the 18th and 19th centuries as having discovered childhood, then we can say that our recent accomplishment has been the discovery of adolescence . . . ."[4] A child's actions have a grace that flows from the security that she is connected to the world and has a clear place within it. She is spontaneous and entirely free from theatricality. Adolescence is the fall from this childhood grace; it is action become self-conscious. The actions of the adolescent are awkward not because of a loss of physical dexterity, but because of a loss of confidence in action itself. Actions exist no longer as givens, but as questions; they become "studied" in the very process of being performed.

Modern art is adolescent in this sense; it is about itself, and can hardly be understood outside the intricacies of its self-reference. "(T)he artist's self-consciousness has come between his conviction and his work, between himself and the conventions (automatisms) he relied upon, forcing him to justify his works even as he performs them. . . . And it means only that the modernist artist is first of all a modern man; . . ."[5] Modernity has become synonymous with the studied performance of its every action, from sex to death.

Admittedly, the awkwardness of modernism, like that of adolescence, can elicit nostalgia for the ease of earlier times, but that misunderstands the causes of the awkwardness. Modernism, like adolescence, arises not from some perverse revolt against a perfectly connected order of activity, but only once that order begins to crumble. It is a response to disintegration, not a cause of it. Thus, in art, the modernist situation is one in which

> an art has lost its natural relation to history, in which an artist, exactly because he is devoted to making an object that will bear the same weight of experience that such objects have always borne which constitute the history of his art, is compelled to find unheard-of structures that define themselves and their history against one another. . . . When in such a state an art explores its medium, it is exploring the conditions of its existence; it is asking whether, and under what conditions, it can survive.[6]

4. Cavell, *World Viewed*, 93.
5. Cavell, *World Viewed*, 123.
6. Cavell, *World Viewed*, 72.

Section II—Transformative Moments

Historically, art had a power in people's lives; it meant to them, captured their deepest griefs and loves. It is only as this power wanes, that modernism in art arises. Only because something which was once possible now evades their grasp, must artists question the tradition and explore the ground on which it stands. Modern art must, of necessity, be about itself, because something that art has safely assumed about itself is in danger of being forgotten. The modernist artist needs to consciously discover something about art, lest it be lost.

Cavell believes philosophy shares the modernist difficulties now everywhere evident in the major arts.[7] Unquestionably, Nietzsche, Wittgenstein and Heidegger shared these difficulties. They viewed their task not as that of producing another intellectual product within the conventional understanding of what such a product is, but of questioning the convention and creating new genre within philosophy.

However, professional philosophers have failed to work this modernist perspective into the understanding of their daily task. Increasing isolation from modernity is the price paid for this failure. Art was forced into modernism because it essentially needs an audience. Philosophy has avoided the modernist task, not because it rests more securely than art in its connectedness to people's lives, but because, up until now, it has rested secure in the university curriculum.

But even this security is eroding and philosophy is in the predicament that it must embrace the modernist enterprise or resign itself to being nothing more than an anachronistic curiosity in humanity's search for self-understanding. Like adolescence, modernism is not a luxury, but a survival mechanism. It is grounded not so much in a distrust of the past, as a fear that something is being lost to the future. To keep faith with philosophy, philosophers must begin a radical questioning of what it is they do. What is it about philosophy that must be consciously acknowledged, if it is not to be forgotten?

Cavell's answer to this question is intertwined with his reflection on Emerson and Thoreau, that is, on American thought before it's professionalization. Academic philosophy's condescension to these thinkers is indicative of its problem.

> I am suggesting that our foreignness as philosophers to these writers (and it is hard to imagine any writers more foreign to our currently established philosophical sensibility) may itself be a sign

---

7. Cavell, *Must We Mean What We Say?*, xxii.

> of an impoverished idea of philosophy, of a remoteness from philosophy's origins, from what is native to it. . . . [8]

Certainly, there are many things that differentiate the writings of Emerson and Thoreau from the standard journal article. Cavell suggests that all these differences are rooted in the way Emerson and Thoreau conceive the scholarly task. They are not primarily interested in articulating a body of knowledge, but in changing hearts or, as Emerson says in "The American Scholar," in furthering "the conversion of the world." They are closer kin to prophets than to scientists.

What is meant by prophecy here? The Hebrew prophets considered themselves as sentries, sounding a trumpet call to a people who were dazed, blind, drunk, reeling, wrapped in deep slumber, with eyes closed and head muffled. Their task was not to propound a doctrine, but to call back from sleep, to open eyes, to warn. *Walden* patterns itself on this task; it too is a call to shake off slumber and wake into a new dawn. Ezekiel's warning trumpet, Thoreau's chanticleer, Socrates' gadfly are different images, but all have a surprisingly similar understanding of task.

Given such an understanding of philosophy, *Walden* can be seen as a model philosophical text. It is not a scientific treatise, but it cuts like a scimitar in every line. It does not inform its readers so much as attack them. And it is precisely in this that it can lay claim to a philosophical lineage. As Emerson realized, "truly speaking, it is not instruction, but provocation that I receive from another soul."[9] It is professional philosophy's failure to offer such provocation that so separates its work from that of Emerson and Thoreau—and Socrates.

Once philosophy is viewed not as an attempt to create a theoretical "mirror of nature," but as the performance of a service, an awakening, the question of its proper audience naturally arises. The prophets were sent to "the house of Israel," Thoreau wanted to wake-up his "neighbors." To whom are philosophers "sent"? What is the proper "audience for philosophy"?[10]

Emerson urged American scholars to "embrace the common," and it is in this spirit that Cavell supports ordinary language philosophy. It is not new words or concepts which are needed, but an awakening to the intricacies of the ones already at hand.

---

8. Cavell, *Senses of Walden*, 148.
9. See Emerson, "American Scholar."
10. Cavell, *Must We Mean What We Say?*, xvii.

Section II—Transformative Moments

But to say that the proper audience for philosophy is common ordinary people is too open to misunderstanding, as if the problems of philosophy could be addressed by an advertising campaign attracting people on the street. Rather, philosophy embraces the common by being about what people as people have in common. The genuine philosophical dilemma is not concocted in academic abstraction, but arises from the ordinary activity of living. It is common because no special erudition is required here, only aliveness to ordinary experience.

Physicists rely on erudition and are in a better position than anyone else to answer the questions of physics, even formulate those questions worth asking. Thus, their proper audience is other physicists. Philosophy is a quite different activity. The slave boy has the same potential as Meno when it comes to doing philosophy.

> What I take Socrates to have seen is that, about the questions which were causing him wonder and hope and confusion and pain, he knew that he did not know what no man can know, and that any man can learn what he wanted to learn. No man is in any better position for knowing it that any other man—unless *wanting* to know is a special position. And this discovery about himself is the same as the discovery of philosophy...[11]

If it is to matter, the subject of philosophy is common experience, and its success depends more on aliveness than on skill or erudition.

Such an understanding raises obvious questions about the propriety of philosophy's place in the professionalized academy. Cavell makes the point that whereas science is quite at home in the university, art is not: "academic art is (with notable exceptions) bad art, whereas academic science is—just science."[12] The work of science exists quite separate from an audience. The accuracy of its data, the precision and comprehensiveness of its theory, are not to or for anyone. Its value does not hinge on response. Art is just the opposite. It is inherently performance and depends for its existence on an audience, however small. Art historians and art critics may be at home in the university, at least if they conceive of their task as doing science about art. But art itself cannot be.

Neither, of course, can philosophy. Inasmuch as it is prophetic, it requires an audience as much as art. Yet, once it is conceived in this way, as

---

11. Cavell, *Must We Mean What We Say*, xxviii.
12. Cavell, *Must We Mean What We Say*, xxvii.

the prophets well knew, it does not fit comfortably anywhere. Sleep is a very inviting state.

> A major motive for wishing to leave the field of philosophy, for wishing relief from it, from one's periodic revulsions from it, would be to find something which could be taught more conveniently, a field in which it is not part of one's task to *vie* with one's students, nor to risk misleading them so profoundly.[13]

What has happened to philosophy is that many have left—if they ever entered—philosophy as prophetic task, for something which fits neatly in the professional academy and can be "taught more conveniently."

There is a recognized distinction between the activity of art and the activity of studying it. The distinction is especially useful in that it recognizes the importance of academic work about art without confusing it with the work of the artist. A similar distinction would clarify the present situation in philosophy. It would reveal that most of academic philosophy (with notable exceptions) is the scientific study of that prophetic activity of awakening embodied in the great texts. Academic philosophy is to prophetic philosophy what literary criticism is to literature. However, literature has not become confused with its study; it is separately alive and functioning as a force in culture. Philosophy is not; it no longer seems to be generating genuine objects of study, but is involved in an incestuous studying of studies. It has forgotten its prophetic lineage, that its proper focus is the common awakening to the common. Only by consciously acknowledging what it is in danger of forgetting can it restore the connectedness to human meaning which historically gave it a place in culture.

If philosophy acknowledges its prophetic character and incorporates this into its daily task, what will it look like? If not the journal article, then what form will it take? This cannot be answered *a priori*. Philosophers will be placed in the same situation as working artists; they will have to struggle to explore old genre and create new ones, so that philosophy can find its proper place in the present culture.

Cavell's own work has been a conscious effort in this struggle; modernism applied to philosophy. While not intending to offer his work as a paradigm, it does provide some indications of what forms philosophy might take.

---

13. Cavell, *Must We Mean What We Say*, xxiv.

Section II—Transformative Moments

A case in point is Cavell's most recent book, *Pursuits of Happiness*. The title seems suitable for an ethics book—an American ethics. However, the book is subtitled "The Hollywood Comedy of Remarriage," and is a study of seven comedies whose plot involves a couple's reunion after separation or divorce. Philosophers will be tempted to dismiss the book as film criticism. Film critics, on the other hand, are not quite sure what to do with it; they seem inclined to dismiss it as philosophy. The book is philosophy, but quite different from the standard scholarly essay. It is philosophy struggling for a new form, not for the sake of newness, but for survival.

But why film? Is this just an idiosyncrasy of Cavell? An attempt to make philosophy trendy by attaching it to film? I think not. In struggling to rediscover what it has forgotten, there is something that philosophy finds inherently attractive in film. Cavell argues forcefully, both in *The World Viewed* and later works, that part of the uniqueness of the film medium is its ability to focus on the "common," in Emerson's sense of the word, to display the grace of the ordinary.

> (W)ithout the mode of perception inspired in Emerson (and Thoreau) by the everyday, the near, the low, the familiar, one is bound to be blind to some of the best poetry of film, to a sublimity in it. Naturally I should like to say that this would at the same time ensure deafness to some of the best poetry of philosophy . . . [14]

Thus, it is not personal idiosyncrasy that puts Cavell's philosophizing in the context of reflection on film, but his conviction that philosophy must anchor itself again in the ordinary. Even the films he focuses on are not "artsy," but part of the common experience of the time. Precisely because film glories in the common, enlarges it, focuses it, does it become an instrument for a new form of philosophical activity.

Pursuits of Happiness is instructive for philosophy in another way in that it conceives of itself as "words for a conversation."[15] Precisely because films are common, they are ready sources of interest and "persist as natural topics of conversation."[16] If philosophy is also about the common and requires no esoteric skills, background, or terminology, then it should be a natural extension of conversation, a conversation that is, in principle, enterable by anyone. If films generate live conversation—and they do—then perhaps philosophy should use them, or at least learn from them.

14. Cavell, *Pursuits of Happiness*, 15.
15. Cavell, *Pursuits of Happiness*, 1–2.
16. Cavell, *Pursuits of Happiness*, 38

Once again, it is a misplaced reverence for the scientific paradigm of knowledge which has lured philosophy from its deepest roots. Science centers on problems, and quality scientific work provides solutions. One should come away from a scientific text with a conclusion. The perfect scientific text would put an end to conversation; the problem would be over, philosophy, on the other hand, is the creation of conversation, rather than the stopping of it. The quality of a philosophical text depends not on the solution offered, but the level of conversation generated each time it is read. The conclusions of Newton can be (and usually are) conveyed in a textbook summary. Philosophy, however is not the ingestion of conclusions from Kant and Mill, but active conversation with them. Each point in a good conversation awakens one to make another and shifts one from slumber into talk. Philosophy is conversation as mutual awakening.

Cavell fantasizes that conversation about film might become as "uniformly good as we expect conversations or columns about sports to be."[17] One needs this same fantasy about philosophy. Again, this is not a call for the popularizing of philosophy, a somewhat redundant notion. Science can be popularized. Because its work is carried on in the labs and journals, its results need to be simplified for the populace at large. However,

> someone who believes in popular, or in popularizing, philosophy . . . believes that the ordinary man stands in relation to serious philosophy as, say, the ordinary believer stands in relation to serious theology—that he cannot understand it in its own terms but that it is nevertheless good for him to know its results, in some form or other. What reason is there to believe this? There is every reason to believe, on the contrary, that this is the late version of one of philosophy's most ancient betrayals—the effort to use philosophy's name to put a front on beliefs rather than to face the source of assumption, or of emptiness, which actually maintains them.[18]

Serious philosophy is not an attempt to construct a system of beliefs, but the activity of awakening, the conversation passionately pursued. Only if professional philosophy reclaims this paradigm and finds ways to embody it, will it achieve an active place in the thought-life of our culture.

One final aspect of Cavell's *Pursuit of Happiness* is significant for the directions philosophy might take in an effort to regenerate itself. At least

---

17. Cavell, *Pursuits of Happiness*, 39.
18. Cavell, *Must We Mean What We Say*, xxvii–xxviii.

Section II—Transformative Moments

since Aristophanes, philosophers have been ridiculed for the unreality of their questions, for their exorbitant efforts to find answers to things no one has, or ever would, ask. The ridicule is not always misplaced. But to insist on real questions in philosophy is not to survey what's on people's minds. Rather, it is to face whatever questions the ordinary raises, once it is awakened to.

Perhaps no problem in the history of philosophy seems less real than skepticism about other minds. As one argues with colleagues, makes love, hassles with bills and talks it all over with the bartender, nothing seems more feigned than to question their existence. Yet, in *The Claim of Reason*, Cavell interprets such skepticism as a deep and common reality, the very source of the alienation at the heart of life. "(T)he ideal of knowledge implied by skepticism with respect to other minds—of unlimited genuineness and effectiveness in the acknowledgement of oneself and others—haunts our ordinary days, as if it were the substance of our hopes."[19]

The fear that is such a part of our ordinary experience, the idea that one never grasps what is going on inside the other or she in me, the extent to which any knowledge of another is a possibility, these are central questions of our age, from the monologues of contemporary fiction to the columns of Dear Abby. To what extent, if any, is actual union-knowledge possible with others? This is a real and common question, the proper stuff of philosophy.

Pursuits of Happiness takes up this epistemological question in a concrete form—marriage. Each chapter deals with a Hollywood film in which a couple break-up and then re-establish their union. Each break-up is seen as a form of skepticism, a question about whether the union of other minds which seemed so obvious at the wedding, is an actual possibility. The epistemological and ethical questions about the limits and possibilities of knowing another are explored as conversations about these common comedies of remarriage.

For example, Cavell reflects on Cukor's comedy, *Adam's Rib*, with Spencer Tracy and Katherine Hepburn. They play lawyers married to each other. The plot revolves around a trial in which Hepburn defends and Tracy prosecutes a women accused of shooting her husband for infidelity. The conversational battle alternates between courtroom and bedroom and becomes, in Cavell's interpretation, a movement illustrating the necessary

---

19. Cavell, *Claim of Reason*, 454.

dialectic of any possible marriage, the way in which skeptical "cross-examination" underlies any human union.

My purpose here is not to pursue Cavell's analysis of marriage, but to demonstrate that his work, exemplified in *Pursuits of Happiness,* provides intriguing possibilities of form for philosophy. It is a sustained conversation on the common experience of marriage/remarriage and the questions that are real to it. In other words, it struggles to break out of the predicament of philosophy. I do not canonize it as the answer, but offer it as the right kind of effort.

Without such efforts philosophy will die, or hang on lifelessly in academe. The task of awakening people to the drama and wonder of common experience and pursuing the conversation which flows naturally—though not easily—from it, will be assumed in other forms; it is too crucial to human self-understanding to die. But the sadness will be that philosophers have isolated themselves and no longer take part in the conversation.

BIBLIOGRAPHY

Cavell, Stanley. *The Claim of Reason.* New York: Oxford University Press, 1979.

———. *Must We Mean What We Say?* Cambridge, UK: Cambridge University Press, 1976.

———. *Pursuits of Happiness: The Hollywood Comedy of Remarriage.* Cambridge, MA: Harvard University Press, 1981.

———. *The Senses of Walden.* San Francisco: North Point Press, 1981.

———. *The World Viewed: Reflections on the Ontology of Film.* Cambridge, MA: Harvard University Press. 1979.

Emerson, Ralph Waldo. "The American Scholar." In *The Essential Writings of Ralph Waldo Emerson,* edited by Brooks Atkinson, 43-62. New York: Modern Library, 2000.

Worlds Worth Wanting
Educating Rita, Stanley Cavell, and the Allegory of the Cave

Anne M. Maloney

Every semester on the first day of my introductory philosophy class, I assign Plato's allegory of the cave. I have yet to find a better way to introduce my students to the activity of doing philosophy. Just describing together what happens to the cave dweller—we usually name her "Sophia"—ends up being a conversation about the joys and the costs of an education.

In addition to the allegory, I have recently added an in-class viewing of the 1983 film *Educating Rita.* This film raises important and provocative questions about philosophy, education, and wisdom, and considers some of the same issues Plato raises, but in a contemporary context. When we discuss the film, my part of the conversation is deeply informed by Stanley Cavell's reflections on Ralph Waldo Emerson, on the *Republic,* and on its allegory of the cave.

My students typically focus on Sophia's ascent from the cave into the light of Truth. They see Plato's vision of education as a willingness to question and be questioned, a willingness to give up our assumptions. To do this, they realize, we must be open to loss—loss of certainty, loss of safety, loss of contentment. They tend to agree with Plato that the loss is less important that what is gained. The ascent toward the fire, the light, into the upper world, Plato tells us, is the upward progress of the mind into the intelligible region where we can behold the form of the good.

My students invariably overlook the fact that Sophia does not "make the first move" in beginning her education. An unnamed Someone Else releases her from her chains. Plato knows that profound change requires encounter with an Other. Whatever Sophia may have wanted from life or dreamed of down there with the shadows, it's not what she gets from this upheaval-minded presence beside her. This mysterious guide grabs her and turns her around; she sees a fire spilling light on puppets, light which is causing the shadows that she thought were real; he then pulls her from the cave altogether, and into daylight, where she sees, not shadows of things or representations of things, but the things themselves. Sophia's education begins in a turning away, but Plato also introduces the theme of return: Sophia returns to the cave because she has been, in some sense, philosophically enlightened.

In discussion, I ask my students why it is that even though she is thrilled with the solidity and rightness of the world outside the cave, Sophia goes back down. Plato's answer is clear; she goes back because she has an obligation, as Plato himself says, "to return again to the prisoners in the cave below, and share their labors and rewards."[1] Now that she has literally "seen the light," Sophia must descend and live again among the shadows; once her eyes adjust again to the darkness, she will see a thousand times better than the other cave dwellers do. Sophia will be able to distinguish the various shadows, and know what they are shadows of, because she has seen the truth about things admirable and just and good.[2] Confident of the value of her new wisdom, Sophia returns to the cave as an act of altruism. Certainly she is in no way desperate.

Stanley Cavell isn't so sure that Sophia's ascent is a climb from the ordinary shadow world to a world of clarity and certainty. Nor is he certain that she returns out of an altruistic desire to bear witness to the beauty and truth she has discovered outside. Cavell proposes that Sophia's discoveries "out there" are—at least in part—what lead her to recognize how uncanny her ordinary cave-world truly is. Sophia's descent isn't so much a return to the ordinary as a turning to it for the first time, but with different eyes. Cavell is less interested in where Sophia's path ends than in where it begins; he says,

> Plato is the one who gave us to think, or the means to think, that there is a return to the cave. But that is a myth. The cave is in

1. Plato, *Republic*, 519d.
2. Plato, *Republic*, 520 b–d.

Section II—Transformative Moments

> us . . . philosophy's return to the everyday is not a return but a turn, not an arrival but a coming-to, a process of coming to, taking steps; a movement that presents itself sometimes as peace and sometimes destruction.³

When Cavell talks about philosophy as a "return to the everyday," a "coming-to," he has in mind Ralph Waldo Emerson's reflections on what Cavell terms moral perfectionism. He sees in Emerson a commitment to the task of finding sources of meaning in the everyday. Cavell says, "I take the opening of the allegory of the cave, which is the opening of the journey to philosophy, to be Plato's portrait of the everyday, the customary public space in which philosophy is first encountered."⁴ It's in the context of our ordinary lives where we begin to think about how we learn to value anything, about what it means to live an authentic life. This ground—the place where we endeavor to become more—is where we hold ourselves up against the idea of a better world, a world that we can partially but never fully attain.

Whatever preoccupied Sophia before her journey out of the cave, and whatever the beauty and power of what she encounters once she is pulled out of it, she returns to the common features of her formerly common life. Cavell again calls Emerson to mind:

> I embrace the common, I explore and sit at the feet of the familiar, the low. Give me insight into today, and you may have the antique and future worlds. What would we really know the meaning of? The meal in the firkin; the milk in the pan; the ballad in the street, the news of the boat; the glance of the eye; the form and gait of the body;—-show me the ultimate reason of these matters . . .⁵

This list, Cavell argues, epitomizes the "physiognomy of the ordinary, a form of what Kierkegaard calls the perception of the sublime in the everyday."⁶ In the *Republic* as well as in many of his dialogues, Plato presents the cave as the place of shadows, where Sophia encounters, not things themselves, not even the models of things themselves; her life has been built on mastering the shadows of the models of the real world. Plato implies that Sophia's intellectual and moral home is outside the shadows where she grew up, and the raw material for her life of wisdom won't be found among them.

---

3. Cavell, *Contesting Tears,* 164.
4. Cavell, *Cities of Words,* 324.
5. Cavell, *Senses of Walden,* 142.
6. Cavell, *Pursuits of Happiness.*15.

Emerson isn't so sure. Cavell acknowledges that in "[E]mbracing the common, "sitting at the feet of the low," Emerson . . . surely takes his stand on the side . . . of the vulgar," [7] that Emerson "[Takes] the familiar and the low as his study, as his guide, his guru; as much his point of arrival as departure."[8] As Henry David Thoreau said in *Walden*, "Heaven is under our feet as well as over our heads."[9] While Plato describes education as a climb from depths into height, Thoreau advises us to settle ourselves, and work and wedge our feet downward . . . "[10] since "'We know not where we are,' and only 'esteem truth remote,' —that is, we cannot believe that it is under our feet—we despair of ourselves and let our despair dictate what we call reality."[11]

Whereas Sophia is dragged out of her cave, *Educating Rita* is a story about a woman who apparently tries to leave ordinary life on her own initiative; when we meet Rita (whose given name is Susan; she has changed her name to Rita after one of her favorite authors, Rita Mae Brown), she is desperate to leave her life of working as a hairdresser, being married to her working-class husband Denny and living among people who know nothing about the "finer things" in life and don't care. She longs for a world of ideas, good conversations, a life of depth and passion and commitment to the things that, as she says, "really matter." Thus has she signed up for a tutorial course in English Literature at the college, and is assigned Dr. Frank Bryant as her tutor.

When Rita first tries to enter Frank's office, she has a hard time getting in; in fact, she has to push and push hard on his office door. She practically falls in; she pushes so hard. The second time Rita comes to Frank's office, she brings an oilcan to oil the hinges, and easily opens the door. Unlike Sophia, Rita doesn't have to be dragged into Frank's world at all—or does she? The answer to that question depends on what we take Frank's world to be. Whatever it is, it certainly isn't making Frank happy. Professor Bryant has come to despise his world, seeing it as false, empty and devoid of meaning. He goes through the motions of his scholarly life, having long ago given up on his own mediocre scholarship. He medicates his way through his classes and office hours with generous amounts of alcohol. Whatever

7. Cavell, *Senses of Walden*, 147.
8. Cavell, *Senses of Walden*, 147.
9. Thoreau, *Walden*, 218.
10. Cavell, *Senses of Walden*, 71.
11. Cavell, *Senses of Walden*, 72.

dreams and passion first brought Frank Bryant to the halls of the Academy, they are long buried beneath a veneer of cynicism and a dull daily despair. He has come to despise teaching so much that he has to drink just to do it, and when he can no longer bear the pretentious prattling of his seminar students, he tells them to leave school and back into the world to "make love, or something."

Whatever inspired Frank to choose an academic life is nowhere in sight. He is a bitter, dried up middle-aged man. It's no surprise that Frank refuses at first to take Rita as his student, responding to her request with a ruminative, "What do I have to teach you?" After just one conversation with Rita, Frank realizes that she has burst through his door already possessing something rare and valuable. Rita may not understand that, but Frank does. Unswayed by his sarcasm and bitter humor, Rita insists that Frank will be her tutor; she wants to change and judges Frank to be the man to make it happen. In this regard, at least, Rita has faith in her own judgment, including—as Cavell says—the judgment of whose judgment is to be listened to most attentively [12]

Rita is ready to leave her world; she is eager to enter a better one, to be his Sophia, and to accompany Frank out of the Cave and into the light. Alas; it may not be that easy. As Cavell points out, education is more than the overcoming of darkness. That darkness—that world of "the meal in the firkin, the milk in the pan, the ballad in the street, the news of the boat"— that is often the place where our education occurs.

Rita has utter clarity about the deficiencies of her old world, but no sense of its value. As Cavell says, "The first step in attending to our education is to observe the strangeness of our lives, our estrangement from ourselves, the lack of necessity in what we profess to be necessary. The second step is to grasp the true necessity of human strangeness as such."[13] If we don't learn how to see in the darkness of our ordinary lives, sunlight isn't going to fix us. Education can't be an attempt to escape ordinary life; it must be a desire to recognize it. Cavell says: "[S]inking roots is not a matter of finding out where you want to live, but finding out what wants to live in you."[14]

The wisdom and beauty in Rita's ordinary life, however, is the last thing she is interested in. All she can see is what she wants to reject and rise

---

12. Hodgson, *Citizenship for the Learning Society*, 194.
13. Cavell, *Senses of Walden*, 55.
14. Cavell, *Senses of Walden*, 157.

above. In Frank, she sees someone who spends his days reading, writing and conversing in an elegant and well-appointed office. Here is someone who knows what kind of wine to bring to a party and how to talk with a proper accent, a man who is comfortable in a world of elegant dinners and refined taste. In her yearning to belong to this world, Rita rejects everything of her former world. Such a choice can come only, Cavell observes, against a backdrop of radical self-doubt, an anxiety so extreme that it strikes at the very root of her being. The price of education, Emerson claims, is loss. There is the loss of a familiar world in which personal significance and worth are securely anchored in everyday rituals and roles."[15] Rita is eager to cast aside those rituals and roles because she wants what Frank has; she wants to talk about things that matter.

What Rita does not seem to notice is that Frank is not, in fact, "talking about things that matter" either. She wants entry into the daylight of his life, but as far as Frank can see, his office has become a pretty dark place. Rita may be entering Frank's office to escape the despair of her ordinary life, but despair isn't a static condition. When Cavell talks about Thoreau's reasons for going to Walden he might as well be talking about Rita: "Going [there] will not necessarily help you out, for there is no reason to think you will go there and live any differently from the way you are going on now."[16] The change that Rita seeks isn't a journey or a task; it is, as Emerson phrases it, a "gleam of light over an inner landscape."[17]

Rita is deeply attracted to the vestiges of Frank's social status. Perhaps Rita sees in him the embers of a love for ideas, great books, plays and poetry. But Frank has lost that vision of himself as a lover, and so isn't sure what Rita wants from him. Yet despite his misgivings, he agrees to become her tutor. In Rita, Frank something that attracts him deeply: her inelegant but penetrating way of getting at and stating things, her uncanny way of naming things and recognizing their value. Rita hungers for books and conversation and art. That world of ideas and of art is a world worth wanting. Frank wanted it once and has lost his way; in Rita, he sees a way to perhaps find it again.

And so Rita and Frank begin to meet in his office and talk about books He begins to show her how to train her voice, how to phrase her startling

---

15. Colapietro, "Aligning Deweyan Pragmatism and Emersonian Perfectionism," 460.
16. Colapietro, "Aligning Deweyan Pragmatism and Emersonian Perfectionism," 70.
17. Hansen, *John Dewey and Our Educational Prospect*, 92.

Section II—Transformative Moments

insights and original responses so that they are less raw. He delights in her wisdom even as he schools her in how to express it in a cultured language.

As their relationship evolves and deepens, such delights between them increase. They are teacher and student, but they are also becoming friends, intense friends. While speaking of couples in his Hollywood "comedies of remarriage," Cavell could be talking about Rita and Frank when he says that they are "achieving . . . a structure of relationship that seems intuitively to satisfy features of moral perfectionism—in their willingness and capacity for mutual education, for transformation, for conversation, intellectual adventure, improvisation, devotedness, for . . . happiness."[18] Cavell's insight is that these romances mark the path out of the cave and into the light, the path from conformity to the decision to become what one is, to fulfill one's capacity for change. Such change requires a willingness to be open to a better version of oneself, and it requires a guide, a friend with moral standing, to whom one is vulnerable and open (it is a reciprocal openness). There is a choice, a decision, at the core of identity, dependent upon *phronesis*, the virtue of prudence. The choice is between life or death.

That is all inside Frank's office, however. Outside of Frank's office, Rita's husband Denny and her father are progressively more angry with her. Denny finds her hidden birth control pills and understands that she isn't in fact trying to start a family with him as he had thought. Even as her personal life disintegrates, however, Rita's intellectual joy increases. We witness that joy when Rita shows up outside Frank's classroom the day after she has been to the theater to see *Macbeth*. She is on fire.

> Frank, Frank, I'm sorry, I just had to tell somebody. Last night, Frank, I went to the theatre. It was fantastic. Macbeth, it was. I bought the book! Oh, it done my head in. I thought it was gonna be dead boring but it wasn't, it was electric. Wasn't his wife a cow? And that bit where he meets Macduff and thinks he's all invincible. I was on the edge of me seat because I knew! I wanted to shout out and warn Macbeth! Well, I . . . I just wanted to tell someone who'd understand.[19]

Rita's joy at *Macbeth* is utterly unlike the demeanor of the other students in Frank's classroom, who prefer to joust verbally about the meaning of tragedy. She is in the grip of the sort of questions that are not, as Cavell says, "alive for one at just any time. And . . . when they come alive, they cannot

---

18. Cavell, *Contesting Tears*, 166.
19. Gilbert, *Educating Rita*.

be put aside as normal questions can be."[20] Unlike the sophisticated and cynical regular students, Rita is transfigured by the power of the play. Frank hasn't seen someone fall in love with literature in a long time, and it lights in him a long dormant fire.

Over the course of the academic year, we witness the joy and companionship that develops between Frank and Rita. Because Rita has become a source of insight and perception, Frank looks for ways to spend more time with her, and invites her to a small party at his home. He cannot imagine that his friends will fail to see Rita's wit and sharp mind, and he is angry when she fails to show up. When they meet the following day in his office, Rita tells Frank that she did come to his house, but turned and left after viewing the party through the living room window. What Rita saw in that moment was all the things she craved and yet lacked, the myriad ways in which she did not—would not—fit in. Rita tells Frank how she knew, in that moment, that she had not brought the right wine, her clothes were cheap and her accent was wrong.

Frank can't understand Rita's reluctance to attend his party; these matters of wine and dress are for him the least important things. Rita responds furiously when Frank casually dismisses those marks of upper class privilege: easy for him, she tells him, to pooh-pooh the civilized and sophisticated veneer of the academic world; he has been bred to that world whereas she is an interloper. Irritated that such things matter to her, Frank asks Rita why she came back to his office at all. Rita responds by telling Frank that she very nearly did not:

> I decided I wasn't coming here again. I went to the pub. They were all singing, all of 'em. Denny, looking happy. He'd just got a few days' holiday from work. And me mother, not really on top form, something was worrying her. Probably me dad. Our Sandra, in love. Her fiancé, about the same. And her mates, all of 'em, singing some song they'd learned from the jukebox. And I thought, Just what the frig am I trying to do? Why don't I just pack it in, stay here and join in with the singing? But when I turned around, me mother had stopped singing, and she was crying. I said, Why are you crying, Mother? And she said, There must be better songs to sing than this. And I thought, Yeah; that's what I'm trying to do, isn't it? Sing a better song. That's why I've come back and that's why I'm staying. So let's start work.[21]

---

20. Cavell, *Senses of Walden*, 151.
21. Gilbert, *Educating Rita*.

Section II—Transformative Moments

At this point, however, Rita's husband, Denny, has had enough. He wants a wife and a family, not a scholar. He tells her, "It's dead easy, Susan—you stop going to that university and you stop taking the pill or you're out." Rita tries to explain: "Denny. All I'm doing is getting an education. Just trying to learn. And I love it. It's not easy, I get it wrong most of the time, but it makes me feel as though I'm in the land of the living. All you try and do is put a rope around me neck and tie me to the ground."[22] Unmoved, Denny tells Rita she must choose: either him and a baby, or College. She tells him she cannot stop her studies, and Denny kicks her out.

Rita has sacrificed a great deal—the chance to have a baby, her marriage to a decent man who loves her, her relationship with her parents. These are not trivial things, and Rita surely knows this. The cost of what Rita is discovering with Frank in that office is real; that she is willing to pay it makes it no less high. She has abandoned her old life in order to claim her education, and she makes it clear to Frank that the only outcome that will count as success is one in which she is granted entry to a new one: "I wanna write essays like those. I wanna learn and pass exams like they do."[23]

Frank is not as sure as Rita is that what she wants is worth what she will have to give up to get it. "I don't know that I want to teach you. What you have already is too valuable." Rita objects: "Valuable? What's valuable? The only thing I value is here, coming here once a week." Frank worries: "But don't you see? If you're going to write that sort of stuff, pass examinations, you're going to have to suppress, perhaps abandon, your uniqueness. I'm going to have to change you."[24] Frank knows that facility with academic jargon isn't worth the loss of her distinctive voice. Rita, however, doesn't see that. Her eagerness to ascend from the cave of her ordinary life has blinded her to its value; it was, after all, in that very life that Rita learned to hunger for beauty and wisdom. In that world, she didn't care if her desire for knowledge sometimes made her look or sound foolish. It was worth every farthing of the cost.

The academic year ends; Frank spends the summer touring Europe with other Intellectuals while Rita goes to summer school. When the Fall term begins, Frank is palpably eager to get back to work. The bleary-eyed cynic is gone; he is deeply thrilled to be studying again with Rita. But Rita returns from summer school a different woman. She is dressed in jeans

22. Gilbert, *Educating Rita*.
23. Gilbert, *Educating Rita*.
24. Gilbert, *Educating Rita*.

rather than in tight skirts and heels; her hair is no longer bouffant; she is no longer wearing makeup. Rita has figured out how to look like a student. She has educated her taste; were she to attend a party at Frank's house now, she would know what wine to bring. Bewildered and displeased by this new version of Rita, Frank tells her that they will spend Fall term studying the poetry of William Blake, only to discover that Rita read all of Blake in summer school. In stark contrast to her reaction upon seeing *Macbeth*, Rita speaks of Blake in a laid-back, almost cynical way. She sounds like all of the other students in Frank's classes. This is not an improvement. It's a terrible loss. Rita isn't aware of it as a loss. Frank, however, is.

Having been kicked out of her marriage and her family, Rita now lives in a flat with a new roommate named Trish. She has stopped working at the hair salon and has taken a job at a bistro. As she learns to verbally spar with other students and put them in their place with her knowledge of literary criticism, Frank becomes more and more depressed. After showing up late several times, Rita finally misses a tutorial altogether and Frank goes looking for her. He finds her in the bistro and confronts her. Why hadn't she told him that she'd quit the hair salon and was now working here? Rita is defensive, recalcitrant, says it doesn't matter. It's just a small personal detail, she says. Of course she knows better, and so does Frank. He tells her that she doesn't have to come to his office anymore, and Rita agrees, convinced that she has found what she came to that office in search of; she tells him, "I know [now] what wine to buy, what clothes to wear, what plays to see, what papers to read, and I can do it without you." [25]

Hearing this, Frank asks her, "Is that all you wanted? Have you come all this way for so very, very little?" Rita will have none of it: "Oh, yeah, it's little to you, isn't it, Frank? Little to you who squanders every opportunity and mocks and takes it for granted." Frank turns on her: "Found a culture, have you, Rita? Found a better song to sing? No. You found a different song to sing. And, on your lips, it is shrill and hollow and tuneless."[26] Witnessing this exchange, we are aware that Rita and Frank are standing in a bistro, an upscale version of the pub she so ardently wanted to leave behind.

Rita's facility with the right words and the right phrases is firmly in place, but she has lost what Frank treasured most in her. This was the source of his delight when Rita countered his "proper" definition of assonance by responding that it means "getting the rhyme wrong." It isn't necessary to

---

25. Gilbert, *Educating Rita*.
26. Gilbert, *Educating Rita*.

Section II—Transformative Moments

put the other student straight about which of Lawrence's works is his best. It is necessary to know that Lady Macbeth is a cow. The Rita of the ordinary life of her cave was extraordinarily original; the Rita who can discuss the correct date of the first performance of Shaw's *Pygmalion* is spectacularly typical.

After this painful scene in the bistro, Rita goes home to her flat; Frank goes to campus and makes a drunken scene in front of the bursar's window, a scene which will result in his separation from the college and exile to their campus in Australia. While Frank is singing loudly and cursing outside the Bursar's window, Rita is discovering that her idolized friend Trish has tried to kill herself. Rita transports Trish to the hospital, and is shocked when she wakes and begins to weep because she realizes that she is not dead. Rita asks Trish why, why she would kill herself. As Rita sees it, Trish has it all. But no, Trish tells her, she has nothing. Trish knows what Frank has always known. If all you have is how to talk and how to seem wise and how to buy the right wine, you are hollow at the core. Trish tells Rita that when she strips away all that stuff, what's left is "just me," and Trish sobs, "It's not enough."[27]

Trish's suicide attempt jolts Rita out of her fog and she sees what she has become. The dull despair of her old world of pubs and hairdressing is gone, but in running from that world, Rita understands, she ran toward the wrong alternative: the dull despair of her new world of bistros and scholarly jargon. Rita comes to understand that she must learn to exist anew in the world while accepting fate and constraint—in Cavell's words, the "rediscovery or reclaiming of the fact of [her] existence"[28]

On the day that Frank leaves for Australia, Rita finds him before he gets on the plane to tell him that she has passed her exams, with distinction. Franks says, "I'm proud of you," and Rita replies, rightly, "I'm proud of both of us." Rita is acutely aware that her education has cost her a happy marriage to a good man and a family; like Sophia, she has lost the capacity to be at home in the cave. She is also aware that her newly won determination to hold onto the cave as a place oddly beautiful and rich with truth will make her unfit for most of the academic world. Every attempt to live in the world of wisdom—the world which renders one laughable and unsophisticated and filled with passion—will wall her off from the "scholarly" world of the university. Rita has nowhere to go.

---

27. Gilbert, *Educating Rita*.
28. Saito, *Gleam of Light*, 5.

When Rita told Frank that she was "proud of both of us," she was thanking him for his ability to hear her remarkable voice, the voice under both the family/pub life and the bistro/academic life. It was Frank's hearing of that voice that enabled Rita finally to trust it. She is at last able to judge the world in her own voice. As Cavell said of Thoreau Rita could just as well have said of Frank: "His problem . . . is to get us to ask the questions, and then to show us that we do not know what we are asking, and then to show us that we have the answer."[29]

As Frank boards the plane, Rita turns to make the long walk down the shadowy concourse and back to whatever life now holds for her. Like Sophia, Rita has, indeed, ascended toward an ideal, a vision of perfecting herself, but as Emerson reminds us, she will not find perfection in any fixed goal or ultimate point of arrival. Rita's best self will always be created in her departure. The pain engendered by leaving is overcome only by the *act* of leaving; as Emerson says, "Our life is an apprenticeship to the truth, that around every circle another can be drawn; that there is no end in nature, but every end is a beginning."[30] In leaving, Cavell shows us, Rita does not find a place to settle down. Rita now understands something that perhaps Plato did not understand—a perfection that refuses final perfectibility. Joy will always be an act of becoming.

"[F]or the child to grow, he requires family and familiarity, but for a grownup to grow he requires strangeness and transformation, i.e., birth."[31] This is what Cavell means when he calls philosophy the education of grownups. It is an endless process of perfection, the process of undergoing the strangeness that is the ordinary. Rebirth is not once and for all, but a 'continuous activity' in the here and now.[32] And the theme of leaving suggests that education of grownups is a continuous process of departure from one's own self and from the other as teacher.

As Rita walks out of the airport and back to her world, she looks nothing like Sophia. Sophia re-entered her cave out of confidence and faith that everything she found outside the cave was better than anything inside. Sophia goes back down because her "mind's eye . . . understands and comprehends [reality] and functions intelligently."[33] For Plato, philosophy's

---

29. Cavell, *Senses of Walden*, 47.
30. Emerson, *Essays and Lectures*, 403.
31. Cavell, *Claim of Reason*, 125.
32. Saito, *Gleam of Light*, 53.
33. Plato, *Republic*, 508d.

task is to give us certainty, and Sophia goes back down certain that she can bring others out into the light. As Rita nears the end of that long hallway, we get no sense of such confidence or certainty. Rita seems unsure, and she pauses; then she squares her shoulders and steps forward. The education she sought—the education of a grownup—has made her less certain; for Rita, philosophy's task has been "to keep the things of the world unsure."[34] Where is Rita going to go? We are left with the question.

BIBLIOGRAPHY

Cavell, Stanley. *Cities of Words: Pedagogical Letters on a Register of the Moral Life.* Cambridge, MA: Belknap, 2005.

———. *The Claim of Reason: Wittgenstein, Skepticism, Morality, and Tragedy.* Oxford: Oxford University Press, 1989.

———. *Contesting Tears: The Melodrama of the Unknown Woman.* Chicago: University of Chicago Press, 1997.

———. *Pursuits of Happiness: The Hollywood Comedy of Remarriage.* Cambridge, MA: Harvard University Press, 1984.

———. *The Senses of Walden.* Chicago: University of Chicago Press, 1992.

Colapietro, Vincent. "Aligning Deweyan Pragmatism and Emersonian Perfectionism: Re-imagining Growth and Educating Grown-Ups." *Journal of Philosophy of Education* 41 (2007) 459–69.

Conlon, James. "Dreams, Madness and Philosophy: Reflections on Descartes' First Meditation." *Budhi* 3 (1999) 169–76.

Emerson, Ralph Waldo. *Essays and Lectures.* New York: Library of America, 1983.

Gilbert, Lewis, dir. *Educating Rita.* 1983; UK; Acorn Productions. Distributed by Columbia Pictures.

Hansen, David. T. *John Dewey and Our Educational Prospect: A Critical Engagement with Dewey's Democracy and Education.* New York: State University of New York Press, 2006.

Hodgson, Naomi. *Citizenship for the Learning Society: Europe, Subjectivity, and Educational Research.* Hoboken, NJ: John Wiley & Sons, 2016.

Plato. *Republic.* Translated by Francis Macdonald Cornford. Oxford: Oxford University Press, 1966.

Saito, Naoko. *The Gleam of Light: Moral Perfectionism and Education in Dewey and Emerson.* New York: Fordham University Press, 2002.

Thoreau, Henry David. *Walden.* Las Vegas: Empire, 2013.

---

34. Conlon, "Dreams, Madness and Philosophy," 172.

SECTION III

Effable Moments
Teaching the Power of Writing

Against Ineffability[1]
JAMES CONLON

IT IS A COMMONPLACE assumption that language has its limits, that there are realities and types of experiences words are just not able to handle. I want to take issue with this assumption and argue that there is inherently nothing that is beyond words and that this fact about language has ethical implications.

It is in the area of religion that words have most often been found wanting. William James argues that "personal religious experience has its root and center in mystical states of consciousness" and that the clearest mark of mystical consciousness is its ineffability. "The handiest of the marks by which I classify a state of mind as mystical is negative. The subject of it immediately says that it defies expression, that no adequate report of its contents can be given in words."[2]

The religious person normally claims god to be a reality beyond anything that words can capture and faith a kind of experience deeper than language can describe.

But it is not just in the area of religion that people make claims of ineffability. It is frequently the recourse of anyone trying to describe realities outside the norm, outside the ordinary scope of human experience. "Words fail to describe" for example "the natural thrill and sheer spectacle of the 450-foot bridge high above Capilano River."[3] Likewise, "there are no words that can describe what is going on in Darfur every day—the kill-

---

1. This paper was previously published in *Forum Philosophical: International Journal for Philosophy* 15 (2010) 381–400. https://forumphilosophicum.ignatianum.edu.pl/index/php?id=961. It is reprinted in this volume with their permission.

2. James, *Varieties of Religious Experience*, 299–300.

3. "Privilege Pass 2009 Tourism Challenge."

ings, the rapes, the burning of villages."[4] And finally, a lover in the throes of separation croons: "I need you now, more than words can say."[5] These few examples give some indication of just how widespread the belief in ineffability is and how many things are believed to fit under its umbrella.

I owe my first doubts about ineffability to my freshman composition teacher. Whenever a student would innocently proclaim some experience or emotion to be beyond words, Father Christopher would be on that cliché like a heat seeking missile. "Don't blame language," he would mock, "for defects which are entirely your own." As my own red-faced embarrassment attested, he was right, at least in my case. Certainly the words I found to express my own sorrow at the funeral of a friend were clumsy and far from what I felt, but Roethke's "Elegy for Jane" had never seemed inadequate to me, nor Auden's "Funeral Blues," nor Thomas's "Refusal to Mourn the Death, by Fire, of a Child in London." I had struggled with my own poetry enough to realize that "There are no words" was most often a way of avoiding the work of finding them, or evading the truth that I did not have the talent to create them.

THE NATURE OF LANGUAGE

When the inadequacy of words is bemoaned, it is usually some form of a representational theory of language that is being assumed. When, for example, parents confront a tragedy like the death of a child, and tearfully claim that words cannot express how they feel, they are assuming that language does a pretty good job of conveying their normal, day-to-day feelings, but cannot adequately perform that function in their present sorrow because it is too complex, nuanced and deep. In other words, language can represent most ordinary things quite well, but fails with certain extraordinary things.

In arguing against ineffability I am going to share in the common assumption that language is representational. However, I will not be assuming that representation is the only function of language, or even its primary one, but only that it is an important, meaningful and distinctive one. There are, of course, many ways in which one thing can be said to represent another. A map outlining an earthen land mass can be said to "represent" the USA. The Stars and Stripes unfurled atop a flag pole "represents" the USA in quite another sense. And, in yet one more sense, the Secretary of State

---

4. Cox, "Horrors Again," B15.
5. Curci and Demarchi, "More than Words Can Say."

"represents" the USA at a treaty negotiation. In what sense am I assuming language to be representational?

I do not believe there is any kind of immediate, one-to-one relationship between words and things. Language is not a picture of reality, even in the logically abstract manner Wittgenstein tried to argue it was in the *Tractatus*. Words are much trickier than pictures in the way that they connect to the world and therein lies their representational power.

Wittgenstein's mistake is worth dwelling on here because the *Tractatus* is one of philosophy's most famous advocates for ineffability, for there being realities beyond language. For Wittgenstein, the most important things in life, things like beauty and goodness, are the very things language cannot touch. Therefore, he concludes the *Tractatus* with a Zen like endorsement of wordless contemplation: "Of what we cannot speak we must be silent."[6] The rest of the *Tractatus*, everything that leads up to that famous final sentence, is summarized by a corresponding sentence in the preface: "What can be said at all can be said clearly."[7] The problem with this is that, in the *Tractatus*, Wittgenstein restricts what can be said to derivatives of simple signs which denotatively "mean" objects in the world. So, he believes that if we have spoken logically and carefully, "there is one and only one complete analysis of a sentence."[8] But, as the later Wittgenstein came to see, "simple sentences" end up being constructed not out of words in their living concrete usage, but out of words as abstract logical symbols. No living, breathing sentence, including the final one in the *Tractatus* itself, can be correlated with the world in the way the *Tractatus* envisioned it should be, at least not without draining it of meaning.

But refusing to tether words to a one-to-one picturing of reality is not to set them totally adrift from it either. The model I want to use for the way in which language represents reality is the way in which dance "represents" music. George Balanchine famously described his choreography as an attempt to get the audience to "see the music."[9] Obviously, he did not mean to imply any simplistic, one-to-one correspondence between bodily movements and musical sounds. Nonetheless, something about the rhythmic interweaving of sounds can be matched (represented) by the interweaving patterns that moving bodies make for sight. I think language represents

---

6. Wittgenstein, *Tractatus*, 49.
7. Wittgenstein, *Tractatus*, xxxi.
8. Wittgenstein, *Tractatus*, 7.
9. Croce, "Balanchine Said," 37.

reality in a similar way. Does it make sense to say that there is music beyond dance? Beyond being illuminated by dance or even perfectly satisfied by it? I doubt it. But is that not exactly what people are saying when they claim to have an experience beyond words? In what follows, I want to argue that the powers we readily concede to language in representing ordinary life, apply equally well to life's rare and dramatic moments. Just as there is no music that cannot be perfectly satisfied by a dance, so too, there are words perfect for every moment.

This can be affirmed, I think, without implying that any sentence, or collection of them, exhausts the moment's possibilities, or is its moment's definitive truth. There is obviously no one "true" way to dance a given piece of music. The number of ways is limited only by a choreographer's creativity. In 1941, Balanchine choreographed Stravinsky's "Violin Concerto" in a dance he called "Balustrade." Stravinsky described it as "perfectly complementary to and coordinated with the dialogues of the music."[10] In 1972, Balanchine choreographed the exact same music quite differently as "Stravinsky's Violin Concerto." Two very different dances can give sight to the same music. Yet, this does not imply that any haphazard way of moving the body would count as dancing to the music. There are clearly dances that obscure the music or miss its mark entirely. The same holds for a wording's representation of reality.

I now want to offer three theoretical considerations in support of my claim that everything can be verbally represented, that nothing is inherently ineffable. The first two have to do with the infinite nature of language itself, the third with the nature of human experience. I then want to draw some ethical implications from the fact of language's inexhaustibility.

THE INFINITY OF LANGUAGE

Language is infinite in at least two ways. The first is that advocated by the linguist Noam Chomsky. He has argued that "discrete infinity" is one of the most fundamental characteristics of human language, and, indeed, the one that clearly distinguishes it from the forms of communication used by other animals.

> [T]he most elementary property of the language faculty is the property of discrete infinity; you have six-word sentences, seven

10. Stravinsky and Craft, *Dialogues and a Diary*, 80.

word sentences, but you don't have six-and-a-half-word sentences. Furthermore, there is no limit; you can have ten-word sentences, twenty-word sentences and so on indefinitely. That is the property of discrete infinity. This property is virtually unknown in the biological world. There are plenty of continuous systems, plenty of finite systems but try to find a system of discrete infinity. The only other one that anybody knows is the arithmetic capacity, which could well be some offshoot of the language faculty.[11]

To Chomsky, language is a system comprised of a finite number of elements (i.e., words) along with grammatical rules for combining them in an infinite number of meaningful ways. Chomsky argues that essential to the syntactical rules of human language is the element of recursion, that is, the ability to embed similar combinations within each other in a hierarchical order. For example, consider the following verse from a traditional childhood song: "I know an old lady who swallowed a dog, to catch the cat, to catch the bird, to catch the spider—that wiggled and jiggled and tickled inside her." Certainly, part of the song's delight is the way in which even children get caught up in the playful infinity of its recursive possibilities. The only way to stop the song is to have one of the old lady's larger meals (usually a horse, of course) arbitrarily kill her off. Because of recursion, human language is a completely open-ended system. Its syntactical rules are such that they can generate from a finite number of word units an infinite number of meanings. This ability of language clearly gives it, as Chomsky *et al* insist, a "limitless expressive power, captured by the notion of discrete infinity."[12]

I simply want to take Chomsky's point about the nature of language and apply it to the question of its scope. If language has "discrete infinity" then it has "limitless expressive power," which means that, in theory, nothing can be outside its purview. If our words are not matching the experience we want to express, the problem must be ours and not that of words themselves.

In this regard, it is interesting to compare the discrete infinity of language with that of numbers. We do not normally speak of there being quantities beyond numbers, beyond what numbers can handle. Although we do use the term "innumerable" in relation to quantities, it is not really comparable to the meaning of "ineffable" in relation to language. When

---

11. Chomsky, *Archictecture of Language*, 51–52.
12. Hauser et al., "Faculty of Language," 1576.

we say, for example, that the stars in the heavens are innumerable, we do not mean that numbers are inapplicable to the quantity of stars, or that numbers are not the kinds of things appropriate to quantities of stars, or even that there are not numbers big enough for that quantity. Rather, we mean that the task of determining what the number actually is, is outside the abilities of the one doing the counting. In other words, with the discrete infinity of numbers, there is no limitation inherent in the system itself, but only in the resources of its users. Should not the same be said of the infinity of language?

Of course, language is not itself a machine that automatically generates satisfactory representations. The tool may be infinite, but the user usually is not. The criterion for determining the right number is pretty straightforward, but not so the right language. Determining the right number is a matter of rote, whereas the right language usually involves some measure of creativity. When are our words the right ones? What exactly is it that we can expect of a verbal representation? Obviously, we do not expect words to be identical with what they represent. We do not expect the word "salt" to flavor our meat, for example, or appear in crystalline form. But if someone says the meat is too salty, and their words are worth their salt, we expect to know what the meat will taste like. There is, however, no easy formula for what rightness looks like in language. Proust can be said to have needed the entirety of *In Search of Lost Time* to catch the precise taste of that tea in which he had dipped a morsel of Madeline cake! Yet, Basho needed only seventeen syllables to catch his monk's quiet morning sip of that same beverage.

When we come face-to-face with the unsettling powers of nature or a searing personal tragedy, our own deficiencies as language users can be painfully evident. But in assessing the capabilities of language itself, it seems important to look at the best creative practices of humanity as a whole and not our own personal resources. How often has some poet taken an agony we thought to be beyond words and put it in all its nuanced form before us? How often have we said of some story: "Yes, that's it; that's exactly what I was feeling." In a similar vein, those who once thought their personal catastrophe inexpressible sometimes find in trauma support groups the right words to make healing possible. To be fair to the possibilities of words, it is important to acknowledge not just those psychological moments when we felt frustrated by them, but also those moments in art or life when they seemed right on the money. Such psychological moments are not, in and of themselves, arguments for the infinity of language's power, but they can provide an emotional balance to our experience of its limitations.

A second way in which language is infinite is presented by the philosopher, Jacques Derrida. While he would not deny Chomsky's claim that language can generate an infinity of possible sentences, he finds infinity in a different aspect of language.

For Derrida, meaning is not a fixed property of individual words (signifiers). Instead, it is a relational property that depends upon the context in which a signifier functions and the interplay with other signifiers in the system. Since the number of contexts is infinite, the number of meanings is too.

> Every sign, linguistic or non linguistic, spoken or written (in the usual sense of this opposition), as a small or large unity, can be *cited*, put between quotation marks; thereby it can break with every given context, and engender infinitely new contexts in an absolutely nonsaturable fashion. This does not suppose that the mark is valid outside its context, but on the contrary that there are only contexts without any center of absolute anchoring.[13]

Derrida's point can be exemplified by both the simplest elements of a language and the vastness of its literature. The letters in any word, for example, have meaning only in the context of other letters. Thus, if one starts with the letter "o", its meanings change as its relationships to other letters change: "to," "of," "ton," "off," "tone" and so on. The meaning is not determined until the relations are.[14] This is equally true, of course, with the relations between words in a sentence. What the word "break" means in a sentence like "John went to Florida for his break" is made clear only in the context of the other words. So, a different collection of words, for example, "John's break will take months to heal," yields a different meaning for the same word. But, of course, this contextual coloring is also true of sentences in a paragraph, paragraphs in a novel, novels in an *oeuvre*, *oeuvres* in an era and so on. "Traces"[15] of every word's past (and future) contexts are hovering around any given usage. Like Heraclitus' river, one cannot step into the same word twice. Each word is a portal on an infinity of traces.

Let me use another example: the word "duck." We tend to think that a word's meaning is anchored in the word itself and that a dictionary can

13. Derrida, *Margins of Philosophy*, 320.
14. Derrida, *Dissemination*, 129–30.
15. Derrida, *Of Grammatology*, 65.

Section III—Effable Moments

provide us with this basic information. Even if the word has more than one meaning, if it is a noun or a verb, this can be handled by the dictionary as well. Derrida argues, however, that any actual meaning, any meaning actually communicated, will depend on the context (time, place, and audience) in which it occurs. Where the word is physically placed, for example, whether it is on a stairway or a cage or a menu, obviously affects it's meaning. Imagine the word placed under a feather in a museum or on a taxidermist's price list. Even a minimal amount of creativity or concrete everyday usage can generate contexts that would endlessly stretch the meanings beyond those suggested by the dictionary.

If the nuances of a simple world like "duck" stretch out endlessly, imagine the rich scope of an historically complex word like "Jesus." What started as the name of an historical figure has become a rich mythological symbol surrounded by hundreds of flavoring stories. What was once a prayer can now be a cry of sexual ecstasy or petty anger. The reach of words is as inexhaustible as the contexts in which they can be placed.

Unlike Chomsky, Derrida does not view the infinity of language as a mere potency, but as something already present in any actual use of language. Classical theory tended to see language as a kind of mirror held up to reality. But the mirror always seemed to fail because there were nuances of reality that the words did not capture. In Derrida's hands, however, this failure becomes a strength. It is precisely because language cannot "totalize" anything, that its meanings become infinite.

> Totalization can be judged impossible in the classical style: one then refers to the empirical endeavor of a subject or of a finite discourse in a vain and breathless quest of an infinite richness, which it can never master. There is too much, more than one can say. But nontotalization can also be determined in another way: not from the standpoint of the concept of finitude as assigning us to an empirical view, but from the standpoint of the concept of *freeplay*. If totalization no longer has any meaning, it is not because the infinity of a field cannot be covered by a finite glance or a finite discourse, but because the nature of the field—that is, language and a finite language—excludes totalization. This field is in fact that of *freeplay*, that is to say, a field of infinite substitutions in the closure of a finite ensemble.[16]

---

16. Derrida, "Structure, Sign and Play," 236.

In other words, there is no way to close off, to stop or be satisfied with, (to "totalize") the meaning of a word. This inability leaves language users frustrated because there are always experiences they can not precisely nail down with words, experiences that seem "more than words can say." Yet, Derrida argues, if we can just renounce such fixating attempts at totalization and instead let words play freely with their contexts, we will find an infinity in the midst of every finite sentence. In other words, if we avoid a single restrictive meaning to the words before us, they might very well include the "more" that we want them to say.

Let me use a metaphor from Yeats to illustrate the kind of infinity Derrida is talking about. In his poem, "Nineteen Hundred and Nineteen," Yeats focuses on the chaos caused by the Anglo-Irish War. Since the horrors of war are often claimed to be beyond words, his efforts are revealing.

> Now days are dragon-ridden, the nightmare
> Rides upon sleep: a drunken soldiery
> Can leave the mother, murdered at her door,
> To crawl in her own blood, and go scot-free;
> The night can sweat with terror as before
> We pieced our thoughts into philosophy,
> And planned to bring the world under a rule,
> Who are but weasels fighting in a hole.[17]

The brutal events that Yeats recounts (a drunken soldiery, an innocent victim, the failure of a legal system) are not unique to 1919; they would be present in any war and multiplied many times over. Numerous as well would be the intellectual efforts to make sense of human history ("piece our thoughts into philosophy") and to establish a universally fair legal system ("bring the world under rule"). Because we humans see our violence as perpetrated in the service of ideals and values, we imagine it to have a nobility far beyond anything that animals could muster. Yet, for all our aspirations and sophisticated weaponry, Yeats finds our violence to rise no higher than that of "weasels fighting in a hole." This judgment by metaphor is delivered with a contempt that is especially chilling. It is also, I want to argue, especially "right" for the way war banalizes brutality, "right" for what war reveals about human nature, "right" for the ultimately venal character of military ambition. But this rightness holds only as long as we avoid locking the image into one specific meaning, only as long as we do not "totalize"

17. Yeats, *Selected Poems*, 109.

it, but let it hang loose and play with its traces and contexts. Notice how richly the single sneaky word "weasel" resonates in this regard. Metaphors are not like mirrors fixating reality, but like dances performed to its music.

By using as my example a metaphor from a master wordsmith like Yeats, I do not mean to imply that the right words are found only in the mouths of great poets. Slang and popular culture can be equally "right." A metaphor like "pissed off," for example, seems a perfect image for a particular kind of frustrated anger. Nor do I want to imply that creative metaphor is the only way to speak a deep emotion rightly. Sometimes a simple account in a poignant context can be achingly adequate to the hurt of a tragic situation. Words can be right in many ways.

As has been noted, there is a longstanding tradition that finds in the infinity of god the paradigm instance of a reality beyond words. In arguing the infinity of language, Chomsky and Derrida seem to turn this tradition on its head by giving language itself a property usually reserved for divinity. Perhaps, however, their strategy is not as revolutionary as it at first seems. At the beginning of his gospel, John clearly and forcefully identifies god with language: "In the beginning was the Word, and the word was with God, and the Word was God."[18] Such an identity, taken seriously, should make even a religious person wary about any quick conclusions regarding the limitations of language.

THE LINGUISTIC NATURE OF HUMAN EXPERIENCE

When people claim that there are experiences beyond words, they are usually utilizing a receptive model of perception and experience. They imagine that the person without language sees the same tree in a field, for example, that the person with language sees. They imagine that the only difference is that the person with language has the value-added ability to give names to the tree and the field. Names enable her to convey information about the tree and field to others without actually having them in front of her. It is on the basis of this model of language that they then go on to claim that humans sometimes receive experiences which have no words adequate to them.

Michel Foucault is one of several thinkers who argue against this purely receptive model of experience. In "The Discourse on Language," he cautions that

18. John 1:1 (NIV).

> We should not imagine that the world presents us with a legible face, leaving us merely to decipher it; it does not work hand in glove with what we already know; there is no prediscursive fate disposing the world in our favor. We must conceive discourse as a violence that we do to things, or at all events as a practice we impose upon them.[19]

We might think, for example, that racial diversity would be present in any neutral observation of the human species, that the world "presents us with" a certain number of clearly discernable ("legible") racial types and that these types pre-exist any verbal schema for their organization. But Foucauldian histories ("genealogies") of the concept of race demonstrate that the opposite is true.[20] The experience of race seems to be more a result of the schema than a cause of it. In other words, we see humanity as black and white only if we are wearing racial glasses, only if we are embedded in a language that utilizes racial categories. Furthermore, these categories evolve not from some neutral reception of the world, but as an exercise of power which one social group uses to validate its dominance over others. Thus, Enlightenment Europeans "invent" the concept of race as a way of justifying their enslavement of other humans at the very time they are proclaiming the dignity of every human being in their own political systems. Humans do not first have experiences and then find appropriate words to describe them; rather, they only have experiences insofar as they are already given shape by words. For Foucault, the very concept of a nonlinguistic or "prediscursive" experience is deeply problematic.

Foucault is willing to agree with Chomsky and Derrida that, in the abstract, there are "infinite resources available for the creation of discourse."[21] However, in practice, these resources "are nonetheless principles of constraint and it is probably impossible to appreciate their positive, multiplicatory role without first taking into consideration their restrictive, constraining role."[22] Yes, language is a "positive, multiplicatory" revelation of the world, but it is first of all "a violence" that we do to it.

Much of Foucault's work is an analysis of the concrete and pervasive ways that a given historical discourse creates an experiencing subject who,

---

19. Foucault, *Archaeology of Knowledge*, 229.
20. McWhorter, "Sex, Race, and Bipower," 38–62.
21. Foucault, *Archaeology of Knowledge*, 224.
22. Foucault, *Archaeology of Knowledge*, 224.

Section III—Effable Moments

in turn, proceeds to do violence to reality by constructing experience according to the dictates of that discourse.

For Foucault, the Enlightenment vision of the individual subject as a free and transcendent user of the instrument of language is no longer tenable. Rather, the human subject is constituted and controlled by language (discourse) and the matrices of power inherent in it.

I think Foucault's work on the constitutive nature of discourse highlights another difficulty with claiming that there are experiences beyond words: human experience itself is inherently linguistic. Once this is understood, it becomes problematic, even contradictory, to talk about experiences to which words do not apply. Words are what make human experience possible. Human experiences come to us linguistically packaged. Since they are made out of words, they can hardly be said to be beyond them.

Some have taken Foucault's position on the constitutive power of discourse to imply a linguistic determinism which leaves the speaker without any real sense of agency. This begets a despair about the use of language quite opposite to my own ethical intentions and, I think, Foucault's as well. Insisting on the discursive construction of all experience need not exclude the possibility of creative expression regarding it.

Michel de Certeau's work is a helpful demonstration of this. While he acknowledges the disciplinary grip that the forms of discourse have on society, he is adept at demonstrating various modes of resistance to this grip, at demonstrating "the ingenious way in which the weak make use of the strong."[23] This resistance is performed not just by heroic poets, but by ordinary people in the practice of everyday life. They resist not by overthrowing the disciplinary matrices of power altogether, but by utilizing them for their own ends. Language use is his primary model for such resistance.

> In the technologically constructed, written, and functionalized space in which consumers move about, their trajectories form unforeseeable sentences, partly unreadable paths across a space. Although they are composed with the vocabularies of established languages, . . . the trajectories trace out the ruses of other interests and desires that are neither determined nor captured by the systems in which they develop.[24]

Certeau's treatment of "Mystic Speech" is an intriguing analysis of such a resistance process. When mystics speak about their experience, Certeau

23. Certeau, *Practice of Everyday Life*, xvii.
24. Certeau, *Practice of Everyday Life*, xviii.

finds a discursive structuring of their experience but also creative strategies for utilizing that structure for their own ends. His prime analysis focuses on a group of sixteenth century texts which were labeled "mystic" and proliferated at the dawn of modernity. Fortunately, many mystics, while proclaiming their experiences to be beyond words, also produced a great quantity of words about them. Certeau's reading of their texts is, I think, supportive of my own claims against ineffability.

He makes clear from the beginning that he is not interested in finding behind the mystic texts "an ineffability that could be twisted to any end, a 'night in which all cats are black.'"[25] He notes that both the geographical locations where the texts were produced and the social status of their authors had been "marginalized by progress."[26] At the very time when the new discourse of science was displacing longstanding religious structures, those displaced were at work creating an alternative discourse. He argues that the mystics, even while claiming the ineffability of their experience, were far from despairing of language's power regarding it. Quite the contrary: "Mysticism is the anti-Babel. It is an invention of a 'language of the angels' because that of man has been disseminated."[27]

As one example of this invention, Certeau examines "the standard unit of mystic speech," a linguistic device he calls "the cleft unit."[28] Examples of this devise would be contradictory tropes like "cruel repose," "silent music," "dark light" and "blissful wound."[29] What such phrases do, Certeau claims, is jar the hearer from her naive faith in the transparency of language, her faith that language directly pictures reality. When this faith is undermined, the reader is forced to look at the signs themselves rather than at what they represent. Since the two represented (signified) realities—cruelty and repose, for example—are incompatible, the reader's attention is directed away from the referents of those words and onto the words themselves. Now, instead of things in the world, the reader sees "wounded words" whose incompatibility creates a kind of "cleft" or emptiness between them.[30]

These wounded words, however, do not depict the failure of all language, but only its rigidly designational form. It is in the very midst of

25. Certeau, *Heterologies*, 82.
26. Certeau, *Heterologies*, 84.
27. Certeau, *Heterologies*, 88.
28. Certeau, *Mystic Fable*, 144.
29. Ahearne, *Michel de Certeau*, 108.
30. Certeau, *Mystic Fable*, 144.

Section III—Effable Moments

exposing that failure that the mystic's meaning happens. "What must be said cannot be said except by a shattering of the word."[31] In other words, what the mystic wants to say, gets said, but its meaning happens in the practice of the sentence rather than its designation. In the very act of shattering the old discourse, the speaker is generating an alternative kind of language usage. "An operation is substituted for the Name."[32] This operational usage of language does not refer the reader to an object in the world, but envelopes her in a mode of experience. This experience turns out to be the very one the mystic is struggling to convey.

The mystic's meaning is, as it were, resurrected from the wounded words. In this manner, the central mystery at the heart of the Christian experience, the mystery of life pulled from the cleft of death, the mystery of absolute fullness inherent in the hole of absence, is figured and enacted in the linguistic practices of the mystics. As the popularity of their texts in the early modern period makes clear, even though the mystics explicitly denied that words were adequate to their experience of the divine, their "paradoxical games" demonstrated something different. "They did not 'express' an experience because they were themselves that experience."[33] Thus by "playing with the mother tongue"[34] the wounded words of the mystics proved adequate even to divine experiences.

Foucault and Certeau are right to call attention to the thoroughly discursive nature of human experience. How could human experiences, even mystic ones, be beyond language, when they are made possible by it? In his poem, "Men Made Out of Words," Wallace Stevens artistically echoes this basic theoretical point.[35]

Stevens begins his poem by asking us to imagine where we humans would be, what our experience would be like, without words. Like the mystics, Stevens has to "play" with the mother tongue a bit to come up with his answer. Without words we would be, he claims, "Castratos of moon mash." "Castratos" would seem to be the plural of the word "castrato," which means a boy who has been castrated to preserve his singing voice. But Stevens surely knows that the correct plural of castrato is castrati, not castratos. Thus, he starts his answer by breaking the rules of language and

---

31. Certeau, *Mystic Fable*, 144.
32. Certeau, *Mystic Fable*, 150.
33. Certeau, *Mystic Fable*, 147.
34. Certeau, *Mystic Fable*, 147.
35. Stevens, *Palm at the End of the Mind*, 281–82.

using an illicit, "broken" word. Next is his use of the phrase, "moon mash." We understand the two individual words, but their union is odd. Is "moon mash," mash made out of moonlight? Or mash made in moonlight? Or by moonlight? Perhaps it is one form of moonshine? The two words seem to form some kind of "cleft unit" in Certeau's sense. Is "moon mash" the song that wordless castrati would sing? Are "castratos" what is left when moon mash, whatever it is, is castrated? The four words leave us with a tantalizing confusion of meanings that conveys rather well, I think, what the experience of wordlessness might be like, managing thereby to prove that even wordlessness itself is not ineffable.

INEFFABILITY AND ETHICS

"But I tell you that everyone will have to give account on the day of judgment for every empty word they have spoken."[36]

There is something encouraging about seeing poets and mystics "play" with language. Using familiar words in ways we do not expect, they provide concrete proof of language's infinite range. But my interest in arguing for the inexhaustibility of language is not merely theoretical. Like my old composition teacher, I want to discourage any retreat into the excuse of ineffability. But while his reasons were pedagogical, mine are ethical. I want to argue that human beings not only can articulate any experience, they have a duty to do so, have, as Martin Heidegger puts it, a "call to the word."[37]

For Heidegger, human experience is as thoroughly linguistic as it is for Foucault. Like Foucault, Heidegger believes there is no such thing as prediscursive human experience. "Only where the word has been found is the thing a thing. Only thus *is* it. Accordingly, we must stress as follows: no thing *is* where the word, that is, the name is lacking. The word alone gives being to the thing."[38] In other words, the realities of the world achieve presence, happen as pieces of a whole, as "things" separated from a whole, only amidst language. This does not mean that a word is some omnipotent *fiat* which "gives being" by making an entity spring into existence from pure nothingness; rather, words "give being" by providing form and meaning

---

36. Matt 12:36 (NIV).
37. Heidegger, "Way to Language," 66.
38. Heidegger, "Way to Language," 62.

Section III—Effable Moments

where there previously was none. "[L]anguage alone brings what is, as something that is, into the Open for the first time."[39]

However, while both Heidegger and Foucault see language as constitutive of human experience and make the history of words a crucial part of their philosophical arguments, their attitude toward words could not be more different. Foucault focuses on the negative and emphasizes the "violence" with which discourse structures experience. Heidegger, on the other hand, chooses positive, gentler words like "disclosing"[40] and "unconcealing"[41] to describe the activity of language. He emphasizes that language is a revelatory power more than it is a dominating one. While he shares Foucault's critique of any one-to-one transparency between word and thing, he finds, on a deeper poetic level, enough revelatory power in language to famously describe it as "the house of Being."[42]

The being that language "houses," however, is not a Kantian "thing-in-itself," nor some mysterious prediscursive entity, but instead, "the meaningful presence of that entity within the range of human experience."[43] The tree that the word "tree" discloses is not the one that falls in the forest when no one is there to hear it, but the one embedded in the history of human interaction with it. In other words, the tree that language discloses is that sturdy green giver of shade, fire, masks and medicine around and under which human life happens. To understand the kind of disclosing work that language does, Heidegger continuously uses poets and poetry as examples. To him, poetry merely intensifies what ordinary language does in the course of its everyday practice. "Language itself is poetry in the essential sense."[44]

Certainly, one of the things that poetry does is take an obscure object inhabiting the periphery of our experience and give it significance in such a way that it becomes front and center to us for the first time. When we experience a new metaphor, when for example Homer describes the sea as "wine dark," we become aware of a connection between those two liquids, sea and wine, that went unrecognized before. A new color, wine dark, comes to exist in and for our eyes. Even more than this, something about the sea's intoxicating powers, pleasures and dangers comes to exist

---

39. Heidegger, *Poetry, Language, Thought*, 71.
40. Heidegger, *Being and Time*, 205.
41. Heidegger, *Existence and Being*, 306.
42. Heidegger, "Way to Language," 135.
43. Sheehan, "Martin Heidegger," 307.
44. Heidegger, *Poetry, Language, Thought*, 72.

in our minds. The effective poet does not manufacture metaphors from thin air, but from the recesses of language and our linguistically constituted experience. Homer's saying that the sea is wine dark does not, as Foucault would have it, violently make it so, but rather discloses its "so-ness" for our savoring. "For appropriating Saying brings to light all present beings in terms of their properties—it lauds, that is, allows them into their own, their nature."[45]

Heidegger's claim then is that all human language discloses reality in a manner similar to that of poetic metaphor. This ability of language makes ethical demands on us. While poetic metaphors are creative, they are not arbitrary. They can be as embarrassingly inept, as they can be gloriously apt. For this reason, Heidegger argues that a certain careful attention, especially to language itself, is the necessary groundwork for all human speaking. "Mortals speak insofar as they listen. . . . This speaking that listens and accepts is responding . . . Mortals speak by responding to language in a twofold way, receiving and replying."[46]

In its essence, human language is neither a denotative tagging of pre-discursive experience, nor an *ex nihilo* construction of it. In language, word and thing, expression and intuition, are equiprimordial; they arise together and are intertwined like music and movement in an improvisational jazz dance. In such a performance, the musicians are as attuned to the dancer as she is to their music. It is precisely their attention to each other that creates, mutually, the work of art. So it is with word and thing. Human speech, if it is to avoid being "idle talk,"[47] must involve a level of fundamental attention and responsibility, a very active "letting be" of things.[48]

I want to extend Heidegger's analysis of our ethical responsibilities to language to include a resistance to any and all ineffability claims. No doubt, human language evolved, just as did the dance of the honey bee, to serve a very practical communicative purpose. No doubt too, the bulk of our daily word count serves pretty much the same purpose as the bee's waggle. However, our distinctively human use of words is not as practical communication, but as fundamental poetry, as a creation of a world and its meanings. Stories seem at least as old as the campfires around which they were told. But as humans, we tell our day to those who care about it, not just

---

45. Heidegger, "Way to Language," 135.
46. Heidegger, "Way to Language," 206–7.
47. Heidegger, *Being and Time*, 211.
48. Heidegger, *Existence and Being*, 306.

Section III—Effable Moments

to provide them with the practical details of our hunt, but the felt tone of its adventure. It is this telling, this saying, that is our distinction.

To become what one is, to be true to one's distinction, is among the oldest of ethical mandates. If poetic words are our distinction, then at no point are we more ourselves than when we are immersed in them. "In order to be who we are, we human beings remain committed to and within the being of language."[49] This means that it is not only our poets who are called to do words' work but all of us who share in the human distinction.

As humans, we are not self-contained units which could be plopped down in any venue. Rather, as Heidegger famously argued, we are "beings-in-the-world," inextricable from our experiential engagement with it.[50] But the world is as inextricable from us as we are from it. The world and its things depend on us for their presence and, as we have seen, this can happen only in language. "The word alone gives being to the thing."[51] This dependence should not be taken to mean that, in some Hegelian sense, things are destined for consciousness. Yet, their "appearance" does rise or fall with us; they can perform their existence only on our stage. To use a choreographic analogy one last time: it is not as if music (reality) *must* be danced to, or was made to be danced to; but it does seem to "shine"[52] when it is danced to, to be more translucent and more splendid in that union. Since the world is a correlate of human language, we all carry it on our shoulders (on our tongues) and should, like Atlas, feel its weight. Any responsibility to be ourselves implies a responsibility to the world. This dual obligation is best understood as an obligation to language.

Now, the most basic duty of those who have human language is to use it, and to use it not just to get by, but to let one's experience be, to let it have its shine in the sun. The texture of the world depends on us speaking it. And if the world is to be sustained in all its fullness, it is precisely those experiences not already fixed in the cliché, that most need saying. While this duty weights heavier on those who have special talents or have honed their skills on the heights and history of literature, it remains the duty of all who gather communally around whatever campfires there are in today's digital world. Heidegger himself would probably be suspicious of the avid

---

49. Heidegger, "Way to Language," 134.
50. Heidegger, *Being and Time*, 78–90.
51. Heidegger, "Way to Language," 62.
52. Heidegger, "Way to Language," 47.

blogger and find in her a tendency to idle talk, but there is something about her determination to leave nothing unsaid that he could not fail to cherish.

So, I argue, we have a duty to words, a call to language. Any recourse to ineffability is an evasion of that call, a ploy to escape our distinctive task of wording the experiences that move us. The world and its things, the language which brings them to presence, the community which both creates language and is nourished by it, are all owed more. Nothing is ineffable

CONCLUSION

I would like to bring this reflection to closure with the example of Dante. He was, arguably, the boldest of human wordsmiths. His *Divine Comedy* is, at its heart, a frontal attack on ineffability. Surely, if anything is beyond words, it is the hell of god's justice and the heights of god's heaven. Even Dante himself twice takes refuge in the word "*ineffabile*" as he attempts to describe what he is experiencing in *The Paradiso*.[53] Nevertheless, he persists in his task of speaking the very things he has called ineffable. In the final canto of his *Comedy*, in the act of describing how much he has already forgotten of his vision of the universe translucent in the face of god, Dante creates—almost off-handedly—a rather remarkable metaphor:

> My memory of that moment is more lost
> Than five and twenty centuries make dim that enterprise
> when, in wonder, Neptune at the Argo's shadow stared.[54]

What this metaphor is intended to illuminate has long been the subject of debate,[55] but I am going to avoid that issue entirely and, following the lead of Joan Acocella,[56] focus only on the image itself, on Neptune's sight of the *Argo's* shadow.

Any understanding of this image must begin with Neptune (Poseidon) himself. He was Zeus' brother, the volatile god not only of the sea, but of earthquakes and horses. A rich history of poems, sculpture and temples has been created in efforts to give meaning to this name. Suffice it here to note that Neptune had hopes that his watery environment would one day

---

53. Alighieri, *Paradiso*, X, 3; XXVII, 7.
54. Alighieri, *Paradiso*, X, 3; XXVII, 915.
55. Alighieri, *Paradiso*, X, 3; XXVII, 837–838.
56. Acocella, "Cloud Nine," 130.

Section III—Effable Moments

be inhabited by those god-revering humans who seemed so tied to the solid ground under their feet.[57]

Next we must know something of the *Argo*. To the Greeks, it was a history creating vessel, the first warship capable of handling the high seas. The boat itself was built by Argus under the guidance of Athena. Since it was reputed to have had fifty oars, its sailing was a complex social achievement. It included in its prow, oak from the Oracle of Dordona. This meant that it was a ship with the ability both of speaking and prophesying.

Finally, in order to begin an understanding of Dante's image, some acquaintance with the ship's captain, Jason, is necessary. He was the early Greek hero who assembled the community of men (Argonauts) capable of handling this powerful ship. His journey to obtain the Golden Fleece and claim his rightful place on the throne of Thessaly was "the first important event in the Greek portion of universal history."[58] His accomplishments highlight not just bravery in the face of natural and political dangers, but organizational leadership and creativity as well.

Once some grasp of these three elements is in place, we can begin to imagine that shadowy shaft of shimmering darkness gliding through the liquid blue of Neptune's realm. The "Earth-Shaker" would not only be astonished by the bravery it entailed, but disturbed by its audacity and encouraged by its future. Truly, an epoch-making moment that is now only a dim human memory.

But notice that Dante, like Jason, is boldly encroaching on divine territory—and in that frailest of crafts: words. Granted, his explicit intent is to compare how little he remembers of his vision of god's trinity with how little humanity remembers of its foundational sea voyage, yet—as Acocella suggests,[59] there is another comparison obvious in this image and that is between Neptune's amazement at Jason's performance and the Trinity's amazement at Dante's performance. On the one hand, Dante is painfully aware of his own limitations, of the gap between god's inexhaustibility and his own inflexible bones. But on the other hand, he has felt in his own pen the inexhaustibility of his craft and cannot help but wonder what awe Infinity itself feels staring into such a mirror.

Nothing is ineffable.

---

57. Alighieri, *Paradiso*, X, 3; XXVII, 837.
58. Alighieri, *Paradiso*, X, 3; XXVII, 838.
59. Acocella, "Cloud Nine," 131.

BIBLIOGRAPHY

Acocella, Joan. "Cloud Nine: A New Translation of the *Paradiso*." *The New Yorker* (September 3, 2007). https://www.newyorker.com/magazine/2007/09/03/cloud-nine.

Ahearne, Jeremy. *Michel de Certeau: Interpretation and Its Other*. Stanford: Stanford University Press, 1995.

Alighieri, Dante. *Paradiso*. Translated by Robert Hollander and Jean Hollander. New York: Doubleday, 2007.

Certeau, Michel de. *Heterologies: Discourse on the Other*. Translated by Brian Massumi. Minneapolis: University of Minnesota Press, 1986.

———. *The Mystic Fable*. Translated by Michael B. Smith. Chicago: University of Chicago Press, 1992.

———. *The Practice of Everyday Life*. Translated by Steven Rendall. Berkeley, CA: University of California Press, 1984.

Chomsky, Noam. *The Architecture of Language*. Edited by Nirmalangshu Mukherji, et al. Oxford: Oxford University Press, 2001.

Cox, L. "The Horrors Again." *The Chronicle of Higher Education* (July 6, 2007).

Croce, Arlene. "Balanchine Said." *The New Yorker* (January 26, 2009). https://www.newyorker.com/magazine/2009/01/26/balanchine-said.

Curci, Freddy, and Steve Demarchi. "More than Words Can Say," track 8 on *Alias*, EMI, 1990.

Derrida, Jacques. *Dissemination*. Translated by Barbara Johnson. Chicago: University of Chicago Press, 1981.

———. *Margins of Philosophy*. Translated by Alan Bass. Chicago: University of Chicago Press, 1982.

———. *Of Grammatology*. Translated by Gayatri Chakravorty Spivak. Baltimore: Johns Hopkins University Press, 1974.

———. "Structure, Sign and Play in the Discourse of the Human Sciences." In *A Postmodern Reader*, edited by Joseph Natoli and Linda Hutcheon, 223–242. Albany: State University of New York Press, 1993.

Foucault, Michel. *The Archaeology of Knowledge and the Discourse on Language*. Translated by A.M. Sheridan Smith. New York: Pantheon, 1972.

Hauser, Marc D., et al. "The Faculty of Language: What Is It, Who Has It, and How Did it Evolve?" *Science* 298 (2002) 1569–79.

Heidegger, Martin. *Being and Time*. Translated by John Macquarrie and Edward Robinson. New York: Harper & Row, 1962.

———. *Existence and Being*. Translated by R.F.C. Hull and Alan Crick. Chicago: Henry Regnery, 1949.

———. *Poetry, Language, Thought*. Translated by Albert Hofstadter. New York: Perennial, 2001.

———. "The Way to Language." In *On the Way to Language*, 111–36. Translated by Peter D. Hertz. New York: Harper & Row, 1971.

James, William. *The Varieties of Religious Experience*. New York: Collier, 1961.

McGrath, Sean J. "Heidegger and Duns Scotus on Truth and Language." *Review of Metaphysics* 57 (2003) 339–58.

McWhorter, Ladelle. "Sex, Race, and Biopower: A Foucauldian Genealogy." *Hypatia* 19 (2004) 38–62.

Section III—Effable Moments

Natoli, Joseph and Linda Hutcheon, eds. *A Postmodern Reader*. Albany: State University of New York Press, 1993.

"Privilege Pass 2009 Tourism Challenge." http://www.vancouverattractions.com/tourism challenge/privpass.html

Sheehan, Thomas. "Martin Heidegger." In *Routledge Encyclopaedia of Philosophy*, edited by Edward Craig, 307–23. London: Routledge, 1998.

Stevens, Wallace. *The Palm at the End of the Mind: Selected Poems and a Play*. Edited by Holly Stevens. New York: Vintage, 1967.

Stravinsky, Igor, and Robert Craft. *Dialogues and a Diary*. Garden City, NY: Doubleday, 1963.

Wittgenstein, Ludwig. *Wittgenstein's Tractatus*. Translated by Daniel Kolak. Mountain View, CA: Mayfield, 1998.

Yeats, William Butler. *Selected Poems and Two Plays of William Butler Yeats*. Edited by M.L. Rosenthal. New York: Collier, 1962.

Defining the Terms of Surrender
Notes on Philosophy and Poetry

Austin M. Reece

"For each man kills the thing he loves, yet each man does not die."
–Oscar Wilde, from *The Ballad of Reading Gaol*

WHAT ARE POEMS FOR? That is a philosophical question. Some philosophers like Richard Rorty argue that philosophy is a kind of literary art.[1] Conversely, Plato judges poetry to be distinct and inferior to philosophy.[2] But as John Koethe states, "Plato's opposition to poetry is thus based on a grudging respect for it and a recognition that poetry and philosophy have enough in common for there to be a danger of one being mistaken for the other."[3] I think that philosophy and poetry are similar yet distinct and mutually beneficial endeavors. Part of what philosophy and poetry have in common is that they "dwell together in some mutual astonishment of words."[4] Put another way, if philosophy begins in wonder at things (including words) and the concomitant recognition of one's own ignorance,[5] then poetry specifically begins in wonder over words and the recognition

---

1. Rorty, *Philosophy as Poetry*, 43–66.
2. See Plato, *Republic* III and X.
3. Koethe, *Poetry at One Remove*, 2.
4. Meredith, *Poems Are Hard to Read*, 45.
5. See Aristotle, *Metaphysics* I.982b.

Section III—Effable Moments

of one's own ignorance in relationship to language. In this way, the poet intensifies the philosopher's awe and focuses her task even as poetry reveals the task to be a never-ending one. Or as Martin Jay puts it, referring to the thought of Hans-Georg Gadamer, "Our finitude as human beings is encompassed by the infinity of language."[6]

*****

I love words. When I struggle to find the right words, when I'm tempted to say that there are no words for what I'm experiencing—the somersaults of love, the sublimity of a sunset, the sadness of a funeral, the outrage at an injustice—I assume that *language* hasn't failed me but that *I* have failed as a language user. As James Conlon puts the matter, "I had struggled with my own poetry enough to realize that 'There are no words' was most often a way of avoiding the work of finding them, or evading the truth that I did not have the talent to create them."[7] To *surrender* in this context means to admit that one is guilty of failing at language in these ways. If hubris in philosophy is the sin of *overestimating* one's abilities and knowledge, then ineffability in poetry is the sin of *underestimating* language's scope and reach to describe and interpret the full range of human experience—if only we possess the fortitude and passion for words.

*****

The *Oxford English Dictionary* contains definitions of over 600,000 words with each one possessing sprawling histories and multiple meanings totaling in the hundreds of millions. In a way, each word is a poem that invites a person to think, to imagine, and to follow their curiosity. Where philosophy and poetry dovetail is in their earnest *paying attention to language*: to the polysemy and ambiguity of words and ordered statements, to language's potential to illuminate and redeem, and in its vulnerability to be misunderstood and misused. The intersection of philosophy and poetry is literary criticism, which is the result of applying the method of philosophy to analyze, interpret, and better understand literary art.

Here's an example of this intersection that illustrates how I construct meaning from experience, how I pay attention to language, and how I want

---

6. Jay, *Fin de Siècle Socialism*, 16.
7. Conlon, "Against Ineffability," 382.

to redeem our abuse of it so that we might fail language, and each other, a little less. Consider the opening lines of an untitled Eileen Myles poem:

> I always put my pussy
> in the middle of trees
> like a waterfall
> like a doorway to God
> like a flock of birds
> I always put my lover's cunt
> on the crest
> of a wave
> like a flag
> that I can
> pledge my
> allegiance
> to. Here is my
> country.[8]

In one context, the words "pussy" and "cunt" are used to objectify a woman by reducing her dynamic personality to inanimate body parts that are treated as a mere means to a man's pleasure. To understand the word "woman" in this way is to do violence to it, and to act on that understanding is to do real-world harm to women. The physical and emotional violence *flows* from the conceptual violence in the prejudiced mind—the misuse of words.

Here is how Myles finishes the poem:

> I always put
> my pussy in the middle
> of trees
> like a waterfall
> a piece of jewelry
> that I wear
> on my chest
> like a badge
> in America
> so my lover & I
> can be safe.[9]

8. Myles, *I Must Be Living Twice*, 150.
9. Myles, *I Must Be Living Twice*, 151.

Section III—Effable Moments

The morality and the magic of this poem is its use of synecdoche, a poetic technique that names a part of something to refer to the whole of it (e.g. "all *hands* on deck," where hands refers to sailors). In this way, Myles subverts the sexual objectification of women—redeeming herself and her lover from the violent use of words—by *reversing the direction* of how "pussy" and "cunt" are normally used. In the poem, those words are used synecdochically to reference her beloved partner, to praise the whole person that she is: "My lover's pussy . . . / is happy / has a sense of humor / has a career . . . / meditates . . . / knows my face . . . / knows her mind."[10] In the poem, her lover's humanity is restored and kept safe from misconception and misogyny. Poetry is the art of choosing the best words and placing them in the best order to say something that must be said. In a lyric poem like Myles', "it speaks from the poet as individual to the reader as another individual, and intends to establish a limited, intense agreement of feeling."[11] By so doing, it delights, informs, and has the potential to transform the heartbeat inside the wound into a signifying scar.

*****

Myles' poem can be interpreted as an appropriation of and response to Marcel Duchamp's last artwork, a life-size installation piece titled *Given: 1. The Waterfall, 2. The Illuminating Gas . . .* (Étant donnés: 1. la chute d'eau, 2. le gaz d'éclairage . . .).[12] *Given* explores the theme of *how to kill the thing you love*. It forces the viewer to look through two small holes set at eye-level in a pair of antique wooden doors, effectively creating a peephole as the sole access to the tableau that lies beyond the locked threshold. What awaits the voyeur is a nude female figure lying on her back in a bramble, holding a lamp. The body rests on an angled vertical axis with the legs spread closer to the viewer while the face in the middle distance is obstructed by the remains of a brick wall. The background is a pastoral scene containing an elevation of trees and the presence of water moving through it above and beyond the body.

---

10. Myles, *I Must Be Living Twice*, 151.
11. Meredith, *Poems Are Hard to Read*, 45.
12. See Figure 1. Mink, *Marcel Duchamp*, 84–89.

Figure 1

Marcel Duchamp, Étant donnés: 1° la chute d›eau, 2° le gaz d›éclairage...
(*Given: 1. The Waterfall, 2. The Illuminating Gas*...), 1946–1966. Interior view.
Mixed media assemblage: (exterior) wooden door, iron nails, bricks, and stucco;
(interior) bricks, velvet, wood, parchment over an armature of lead, steel, brass,
synthetic putties and adhesives, aluminum sheet, welded steel-wire screen, and wood;
Peg-Board, hair, oil paint, plastic, steel binder clips, plastic clothespins, twigs, leaves,
glass, plywood, brass piano hinge, nails, screws, cotton, collotype prints, acrylic

Section III—Effable Moments

varnish, chalk, graphite, paper, cardboard, tape, pen ink, electric light fixtures, gas lamp (Bec Auer type), foam rubber, cork, electric motor, cookie tin, and linoleum
7 feet 11 1/2 inches × 70 inches × 49 inches (242.6 × 177.8 × 124.5 cm)
Philadelphia Museum of Art: Gift of the Cassandra Foundation, 1969
1969-41-1
© Artists Rights Society (ARS), New York / ADAGP, Paris / Estate of Marcel Duchamp

The title of the artwork—*Given*—signifies on at least three levels. The first is how the artwork operates on perception. Because of the constraints set up by Duchamp (peephole, locked doors, brick wall), the viewer is only offered one adumbration of a scene where a crucial detail, the woman's face, is left out of view. Because of this lack of access, we don't know if she is alive or dead, experiencing pleasure or pain, looking toward the human viewer or away at the trees, forming a word with her mouth or slack-jawed. What is given is complicated by what is not given.[13] A definitive, all-encompassing description of the artwork is suspended even as the viewer is invited to imagine what's left out just beyond their perceptual gaze.

This invitation to imagine and think leads the viewer into the second level of signification. Thinking itself, conceiving, is not reducible to the passive reception of perceptible data. Even if the doors were to open and we were allowed to step past the brick wall to examine every angle of the body to form a complete picture, we would still be lacking something essential to the human *qua an integral whole*. Put another way, an autopsy cannot capture the human capacities for rational and emotional intelligence, for innovative language use, for free action in the form of faith, desire, and rebellion that can shape a person in unforeseen ways. A human *subject* cannot be fully circumscribed as a perceptual *object*.

With this distinction in mind, it's possible to interpret the artwork as a murder scene where the body has been *posed* by the killer to *imitate agency* where in fact it has been utterly destroyed—dehumanization *par excellence*. Posing, as a category of forensic criminal analysis, denotes when a murder scene is altered for the sole purpose of serving the fantasy of the killer.[14] Tellingly, both Jack the Ripper and the Black Dahlia killer posed their female victims with the legs spread as Duchamp has done here.[15]

As Simon Critchley points out, imagination is distinct from fancy: imagination pictures things as they were (in memory), as they are (in

---

13. See Judovitz, *Unpacking Duchamp*, 195–225.
14. Geberth, "Frequency of Body Posing in Homicides."
15. See Epstein, *Annals of Unsolved Crime*, 139–43; 151–54.

mental representations of perceptual data), and even beyond us as they might otherwise be (through novel combination and connection); fancy fantasizes about things that are not and could never be (or should never be): zombies, vampires, and women as two-dimensional sexual objects to be possessed and posed.[16] Fantasy is pure escape from reality, while imagination is potentially exodus—a way forward that recognizes where we've been and what we need to change in order to survive and exist within our limits. The third level of signification of *Given* moves beyond interpreting the artwork as a posed murder scene to critical reflection of the inner workings of the male fantasy of female beauty and its potentially murderous implications. Put another way, *Given* gives the gift of provocation to ponder a pervasive phenomenon in life and art, namely how and why someone can figuratively "kill the thing they love" by first failing at language—a preventable *death in life*.

*****

It's at this point that I want to propose a structural analogy between Emmanuel Lévinas' interpretation of the human face as the site of transcendence and ethical responsibility and the *face of the word*. Lévinas describes the face as follows:

> The approach to the face is the most basic mode of responsibility. As such, the fact of the other is verticality and uprightness; it spells a relation of rectitude. The face is not in front of me but above me; it is the other before death, looking through and exposing death. [. . .] Thus the face says to me: you shall not kill. [. . .] My ethical relation of love for the other stems from the fact that the self cannot survive by itself alone, cannot find meaning within its own being-in-the-world, within the ontology of sameness.[17]

Analogously, a person's relationship to language can be interpreted as a mode of responsibility. The face of the word symbolizes the site of a word's potential for polysemy and modulation, for exponential shifts of meaning in ever evolving contexts. In this way, the word stands in a vertical position above any person's current usage—transcending the attempt to monopolize any one meaning over the others. This monopolization qua oversimplification of a word's polysemous nature represents the death of the word. The

---

16. Critchley, *Things Merely Are*, 11.
17. Lévinas, "Ethics of the Infinite," 189.

Section III—Effable Moments

word is "de-faced"[18] in this way, which acts as the progenitor for other kinds of disfigurement so brilliantly symbolized in Francis Bacon's infamous portraits that injure its faces[19] and in Duchamp's *Given* where the nude's face is removed altogether. It's precisely here where Myles' poem finds its counterpointed voice to sing her song of love. Her lover is placed up in a tree as opposed to Duchamp's lover who is placed in a thicket on the ground; her lover is placed in a waterfall while Duchamp's lover is placed on dry ground out of reach of the idyllic waterfall above and behind her; her lover's dynamic personality is protected in and through language while Duchamp's lover is posed corpselike, de-faced, and forever silent. The poet hears[20] and heeds the call to let words live in their full range of signification which is her responsibility as a lover of language.

*****

Shannon Franklin's artwork titled *Object*, a three-tiered rock-like installation that supports a grasping hand while small but significant objects lie below it out of reach, is both a compelling and creative representation of thwarted female agency and a terrifyingly open grave of guilt.[21]

---

18. See Lévinas, *Is It Righteous To Be*, 246.

19. For an example, see Bacon, *Three Studies of Muriel Belcher* (1966) in Ficacci, *Francis Bacon*, 71.

20. Besides form and analogy, tone is considered one of the central features of any poem. Tone can be defined as the expression on the *face* of the word. Thus, the poet is attuned to transient shifts in tone while the one who is guilty of misusing words by defacing them is tone-deaf. See Spiegelman, *How to Read and Understand Poetry*.

21. See Figure 2. It's almost as if the hand is reaching out from its earthly grave, not in resurrection, but in desperation and surrender. Its nihilism (that *nothing* exists outside its grasp) has led to its embodied solipsism, i.e. that it exists *totally alone* in a world it is responsible for emptying. What Franklin maps with tactile precision as a rock-like tomb might also be imagined as "an inclined beach sliding toward a dreadful sea." Either way, the hand's guilt is *apocalyptic*. See Wallace, "The Empty Plenum," in *Both Flesh and Not Essays*, 77–78.

Figure 2

Shannon Franklin, *Object,* 2018
Plaster, wood, and urethane foam, 4' tall, 6'4" wide, and 3'6" deep, Private Collection,
Photo courtesy of the artist

As in Myles' poem above, the hand in Franklin's piece has a range of synecdochical registers. The hand is both severed from its body and removed from its context, yet it evokes "in such a way as to cause a kind of explosion of associative connections within the recipient" that "feels sudden and percussive, like the venting of a long-stuck valve."[22] The hand, at once an accomplished rendering of the hand that raped Proserpina in Bernini's masterwork, also brings to mind the dismemberment of Orpheus at the hands of the maenads. Pausanias conjectures that Orpheus may have actually committed suicide by his own hand over the grief and guilt of losing his beloved Eurydice to the Underworld because of *his own acknowledged failure,* i.e. he looked back.[23] *Object* explores the defacements involved in sexism, racism, and classism[24] while staging the heartbreaking scene of

22. Wallace, *Consider the Lobster,* 61.

23. See Pausanias, *Description of Greece,* Chapter 29, Section 9.

24. If the tiered layers of sedimentation represent the racist, classist, and sexist history of oppressive practices that hold up the hand, the rock-like structure simultaneously crushes a woman beneath it. The power of imagination, the poetic impulse to play with

the *aftermath* of these defacements—the consequences of conceptual and mythological violence turned outwards and, not to be overlooked, *inwards* toward the victimizing male hand itself: traumatic loss, guilt, pathological mourning, and suicide. Robert Lowell's stunning lines of poetry in "Skunk Hour" come to mind here: "My mind's not right . . . // I hear / my ill-spirit sob in each blood cell, / as if my *hand* were at its throat . . . / I myself am hell."[25]

*****

The one shared characteristic of normal and pathological mourning is the phenomenon of traumatic loss that causes both to initiate their dynamic processes in response. Psychic trauma is not simply a mental wound as opposed to a physical one, but an "inexperienced experience"[26] caused by "overwhelming affect"[27] resulting in a "time of no time."[28] Intrusive, destructive, and repetitive thoughts and feelings characterize psychic trauma if left to worsen without treatment. From Freud onward, psychic trauma describes the mind in a state of serious injury where its vital integrity is in danger. A survivor of a cataclysmic train derailment, a soldier returning from an inhumane war, a victim of child sexual abuse, and like Orpheus, a person failing their beloved spouse and thereby losing them forever—these are classic case studies of psychic trauma that invite the interpreter to look beneath the surface pain to the psychological mechanisms at work below. Given their violent origins, psychic traumas appear as open wounds that seemingly never close on their own, continuously interrupting the self.[29] From a practical standpoint, a person's spontaneous freedom to act in the world is undermined by trauma.[30] The traumatized self can be likened to a piece of glass dropped from a great height. The notion of *shattering* is

---

language, the artistic impulse to shape our fears and desires, make it possible to scale the sheer rock wall of prejudice and its abuses of language, or blow a hole through it. Put another way, if the violence of prejudice is a mountain range of pain running through human history, endlessly dividing us from each other and dividing us from who we could become, then the artwork, the poem—the place where words live—is a hidden door in the forbidding rock.

25. Lowell, *Life Studies and For the Union Dead,* 95. Emphasis added.
26. Kearney, "Writing Trauma," 7–28.
27. Stolorow, *Trauma and Human Existence,* 23.
28. Riley, *Time Lived,* 12.
29. Kearney, "Writing Trauma," 8.
30. Westphal, *Kierkegaard and Levinas in Dialogue,* 81.

commonly used in trauma studies to describe affected persons and the new world of post-traumatic subjectivity itself—a world frozen in time and stripped of possibility.

An *inexperienced experience* suggests a scenario where a person is involved in a significantly injurious event that cannot be processed or understood in the present and thereby cannot be remembered at a future time. Despite the person's direct involvement and their concomitant pain, the event exists on a plane of unconsciousness or at least in the "untouristed parts of one's consciousness."[31] Paradoxically trauma undermines memory while tethering the person to the past. For the traumatized person, time is elastic: it marches on so fast and then in an instant, triggered by a smell or a photograph, they are snapped back to a moment like no time has passed to relive the violence.

The work of mourning involves working through the loss of a loved one, which can be facilitated by the sublimation and catharsis that poetry potentially provides. *Pathological* mourning, in the forms of mania and melancholia, occurs when healthy mourning is interrupted by guilt, which leads to self-destruction.[32] The melancholic, in particular, has lost their sense of wonder and astonishment. They believe that nothing good can come out of the future and that no word could redeem or forgive them. They're divided between who they thought they were and who they have become—irrevocably guilty. When the melancholic commits suicide they imagine they're committing homicide, i.e. *they're killing the hated other that they've become.*[33]

*****

For me, the most poignant detail of Franklin's *Object* is the inclusion of a single phrase inscribed on an apple scattered far below the outstretched hand— τῇ καλλίστῃ (*tei kallistei*)—meaning *the most beautiful*.[34] A concept is an idea in the mind with (con-) which we use to grasp and capture (-cept) some aspect of the world and our place within it. Perhaps the severed hand is the grasping concept and the carved apple a symbol of that which lies beyond it—both the human face and the face of the word, waiting to be written. Perhaps this is what is most beautiful—that the hand cannot en-

---

31. DeLillo, *Unpublished Letter to David Foster Wallace.*
32. Freud, "Mourning and Melancholia," 20–21.
33. Critchley, *How to Stop Living and Start Worrying*, 67.
34. See Figure 3. West, *Greek Epic Fragments*, 80–81.

close itself around beauty, or make a final judgment about it. As soon as it does, it loses the words coming out of the future to astonish, enlighten, and extend the horizon of the concept.[35] As soon as it does, it finds itself guilty of failing at language—a guilt that may initiate the destructive logic of pathological mourning or may be covered over and resisted by the manic certainty that the meaning it possesses is the only meaning possible.

Figure 3
Shannon Franklin, *Object* (Detail), *His Trophy* (Apple), 2018, Plaster, wood, and urethane foam, 4' tall, 6'4" wide, and 3'6" deep, Private Collection,
Photo courtesy of the artist.

But as John Berger notes in "The Hour of Poetry", "To break the silence of events, to speak of experience however bitter or lacerating, to put into words, is to discover the hope that these words may be heard [. . .]."[36] And he concludes, "Poetry is addressed to language itself."[37] How? The poem

---

35. As Bruns states, "The principle is that the extension of any concept cannot be closed by a frontier. [. . .] *The poem forces us to expand our boundaries of what we think of as meaningful.*" The poem and the thinking it requires provide an opportunity to co-construct the meaning from the experience of the poem and its innovative use of language. This is a call to dialogue and relationship that potentially breaks the solipsistic spell. See Bruns, *Material of Poetry*, 27.

36. Berger, *Selected Essays of John Berger*, 452.

37. Berger, *Selected Essays of John Berger*, 450.

laments the loss of words even as it stutters and stumbles on new words to continue the labor of *reassembling what has been scattered*.[38]

*****

I want to conclude with a poem of my own titled "Surrender."[39] It attempts to think through a crude analogy, namely, as a maimed limb requires a prosthetic to function again, the broken heart or split mind needs the poem as a *figurative* prosthetic to move beyond its grief and guilt.

> Prosthesis for someone
> who's lost his mind
> hides the quiet
> of her never-coming-back:
> bruised-black, bled-white—*these lines*.
> His upturned heart's
> soon a ruin
> without it. Still
> there are propinquities: a close
> reading of her last email
> before she died
> hurts the same every time. Still
> the dead are dead, and the rest
> go limping on. Guilt,
> like water, works under and washes away
> the ground. *This poem*—a cleft nub
> of stretched red skin
> that keeps reaching
> for words . . .
>
> O Reader,
> please look into my tired face.
> Can't you see
> this is me
> with my hands up?

---

38. Berger, *Selected Essays of John Berger*, 450.
39. This poem is dedicated to Saron Harford.

SECTION III—EFFABLE MOMENTS

BIBLIOGRAPHY

Aristotle. *Metaphysics Books 1-9*. Loeb Classical Library 271. Translated by Hugh Tredennick. Cambridge: Harvard University Press, 1922.

Berger, John. *Selected Essays of John Berger*. Edited by Geoff Dyer. New York: Vintage International, 2001.

Bruns, Gerald L. *The Material of Poetry: Sketches for a Philosophical Poetics*. Athens, GA: University of Georgia Press, 2005.

Conlon, James. "Against Ineffability." In *Forum Philosophicum: International Journal for Philosophy* 15 (2010) 380-400.

Critchley, Simon. *How to Stop Living and Start Worrying*. Cambridge: Polity, 2010.

———. *Things Merely Are: Philosophy in the Poetry of Wallace Steven*. New York: Routledge, 2005.

DeLillo, Don. *Unpublished Letter to David Foster Wallace*. The Harry Ransom Center, The University of Texas, Folder 101.10, dated November 6, 1996.

Duchamp, Marcel. *Given: 1. The Waterfall, 2. The Illuminating Gas* . . . Philadelphia Museum of Art.

Epstein, Edward Jay. *The Annals of Unsolved Crime*. Brooklyn: Melville House, 2013.

Ficacci, Luigi. *Francis Bacon 1909-1992: Deep Beneath the Surfaces of Things*. Köln: Taschen, 2015.

Franklin, Shannon. *Object*. Private collection.

Freud, Sigmund. "Mourning and Melancholia." In *On Freud's "Mourning and Melancholia,"* edited by L. Glocer Fiorini, et al. 16–34. London: Karnac, 2007.

Geberth, Vernon. "Frequency of Body Posing in Homicides." *Law and Order* (February 2010). http://www.hendonpub.com/resources/article_archive/results/details?id=1866.

Jay, Martin. *Fin de Siècle Socialism and Other Essays*. New York: Routledge, 1988.

Judovitz, Dalia. *Unpacking Duchamp: Art in Transit*. Berkeley: University of California Press, 1995.

Kearney, Richard. "Writing Trauma: Narrative Catharsis in Homer, Shakespeare and Joyce." In *Giornale di metafisca* 1 (2013) 7–28.

Koethe, John. *Poetry at One Remove: Essays*. Ann Arbor: University of Michigan Press, 2000.

Lévinas, Emmanuel. "Ethics of the Infinite." In *States of Mind: Dialogues with Contemporary Thinkers*, edited by Richard Kearney 177–200. New York: New York University Press, 1995.

———. *Is It Righteous To Be?: Interviews with Emmanuel Levinas*. Edited by Jill Robbins. Stanford: Stanford University Press, 2001.

Lowell, Robert. *Life Studies and For the Union Dead*. New York: Farrar, Straus and Giroux, 2007.

Meredith, William. *Poems Are Hard to Read*. Ann Arbor: University of Michigan Press, 1991.

Mink, Janis. *Marcel Duchamp 1887-1968: Art as Anti-Art*. Köln: Taschen, 2016.

Myles, Eileen. *I Must Be Living Twice: New and Selected Poems*. New York: Ecco, 2015.

Pausanias. *Description of Greece, Volume I: Books 1-2*. Loeb Classical Library 92. Translated by W.H.S. Jones. Cambridge, MA: Harvard University Press, 1918.

Plato. *Republic*. Translated by G.M.A. Grube. Indianapolis: Hackett, 1992.

Rorty, Richard. *Philosophy as Poetry*. Charlottesville: University of Virginia Press, 2016.

Riley, Denise. *Time Lived, Without Its Flow.* London: Capsule, 2012.

Spiegelman, Willard. *How to Read and Understand Poetry.* Chantilly, VA: Teaching Company, 1999.

Stolorow, Robert. *Trauma and Human Existence: Autobiographical, Psychoanalytic, and Philosophical Reflections.* New York: Analytic, 2007.

Wallace, David Foster. *Both Flesh and Not Essays.* New York: Back Bay, 2013.

———. *Consider the Lobster And Other Essays.* New York: Back Bay, 2006.

West, Martin L. *Greek Epic Fragments: From the Seventh to the Fifth Centuries BC.* Loeb Classical Library 497. Cambridge, MA: Harvard University Press, 2003.

Westphal, Merold. *Kierkegaard and Levinas in Dialogue.* Bloomington: Indiana University Press, 2008.

Wilde, Oscar. *The Ballad of Reading Gaol and Other Poems.* New York: Dover, 1992.

SECTION IV

Pragmatic Moments
Just Teaching in America

Cornel West's Socratic Understanding of America[1]

JAMES CONLON

IN *THE AMERICAN EVASION of Philosophy*, Cornel West praises American pragmatist thinkers precisely because they were able to avoid the narrow epistemological focus of European philosophy and engage instead in a "future oriented instrumentalism that tries to deploy thought as a weapon to enable more effective action."[2] Analyzing a line of thinkers that runs from Emerson, through Du Bois, to Rorty, West argues that in America, philosophical thinking becomes "a continuous cultural commentary or set of interpretations that attempt to explain America to itself at a particular historical moment."[3] West places his own thinking in this lineage and sees himself as engaged in a similar, intensely practical effort at national self-understanding.

This means that West's intellectual work is unabashedly immersed in America and its meanings. At least ten of his books refer to America somewhere in their title or subtitle. In these books, he does not just analyze America's social and cultural environment, but utilizes its character traits in his ethical explorations. His ideals are developed in agonistic dialogue with American values and directed specifically at challenging American citizens to a more complete humanity. He is unashamedly clear about his focus on nationality. "One of the central aims of my work, since *Prophecy*

---

1. A different version of this paper was published under the title "Cornel West's Pragmatic Understanding of America" in *The Journal of Black Studies* (October 11, 2016). Sage Publishing gave the author permission to publish this earlier version of the paper in this volume.
2. West, *American Evasion of Philosophy*, 5.
3. West, *American Evasion of Philosophy*, 4.

Section IV—Pragmatic Moments

Deliverance! has been to examine critically the soul of American civilization—its distinctive institutions, practices, and ideas—in order to disclose its democratic possibilities."[4] A similar focus on practicality, West argues, is found not just in American philosophy and thought, but in Socrates as well. In West's eyes, Socrates believed "it was his central mission to combat the corruptions of elite power by questioning the narrow ideological and prejudicial thinking of his day."[5] In this, Socrates prefigured the democratic energies of American Pragmatism. West's own national focus, therefore, puts him not only in the footsteps of American Pragmatism, but in the pragmatic footsteps of Socrates.

West's focus on nationality is an exception among contemporary philosophers. In fact, the increasing globalization of the twentieth century has led philosophers like Martha Nussbaum and Kwame Anthony Appiah to emphasize cosmopolitan values rather than national ones. Nussbaum argues, for example, that no ethical priority should be given to national allegiance. According to her, children should be educated to see themselves "above all" as citizens of the world rather than of some local region or country.[6]

While not unmindful of cosmopolitan values, most of West's intellectual energies are employed in understanding America. Like Socrates, he is one of his homeland's severest critics, but also, like Socrates, one of its profoundest lovers. His book with R.M.Unger, *The Future of American Progressivism*, concludes as follows:

> To understand your country you must love it. To love it you must, in a sense, accept it. To accept it as it is, however, is to betray it. To accept your country without betraying it, you must love it for that in it which shows what it might become. America . . . needs citizens who love it enough to reimagine and remake it.[7]

West is clearly a citizen devoted to understanding his country in precisely this way. This paper will examine some of the aspects of West's understanding of America.

---

4. West, "Afterward," 350.
5. West, *Democracy Matters*, 208.
6. Nussbaum, "Liberal Education and Global Community," 42–47.
7. Unger and West, *Future of American Progressivism*, 92.

AMERICAN CIVILIZATION

West's grasp of "American civilization—its distinctive institutions, practices and ideas" is extraordinarily broad and he has analyzed its various aspects on many levels. In *The Cornel West Reader*, for example, he has essays on Americans as diverse as Walt Whitman, Jackie Robinson, and Marvin Gaye. His topics cover an equally broad range from "The Crisis in Contemporary American Religion," to "Parents and National Survival." Fortunately for the student of his work, he is fond of summaries, lists, and repetition. In *The Evasion of Philosophy* he offers the following five characteristics as

> distinctive features of American civilization: its revolutionary beginning combined with a slave-based economy; its elastic liberal rule of law combined with an entrenched business-dominated status quo; its hybrid culture in combination with a collective self-definition as homogeneously Anglo-American; its obsession with mobility, contingency, and pecuniary liquidity combined with a deep moralistic impulse; and its impatience with theories and philosophies alongside ingenious technological innovation, political strategies of compromise, and personal devices for comfort and convenience.[8]

These five qualities are not intended to be definitive, and are not offered in the spirit of any essentialist enterprise. They provide an excellent example, however, of West's Socratic philosophizing. They arise from someone "deeply shaped by American civilization, but not fully a part of it."[9] In other words, although he sees himself as a thoroughly American product, his blackness means he has never been fully embraced by official America as American.

The five features West presents are not qualities as such, but paradoxes. In this they reflect the paradoxicality of the observer himself as Black American. Each of the five can be linked to more extensive treatments somewhere else in his oeuvre and each could serve as an intriguing starting point for cultural reflection. They are not simply a tabulation of strengths and weaknesses, but are formulated in such a way that a specific strength and a specific weakness play questioningly off each other. This makes them especially effective in generating philosophical reflection on the meanings

---

8. West, *American Evasion of Philosophy*, 5.
9. West, *American Evasion of Philosophy*, 8.

Section IV—Pragmatic Moments

behind the details. Let me focus on two of these characteristic paradoxes as examples.

The first is that America's revolutionary beginning is founded on a slave-based economy. This contradictory combination of visionary ideals with brutal, reactionary practices is a constant theme in West's work. He clearly values the revolutionary spirit involved in creating the American nation, its political founding. Both the zeal of the early settlers to experiment with new forms of community and the democratic ideals of the Founding Fathers are genuine sources of instruction and inspiration for him. However, he never considers these ideals in isolation from the blindly vicious aspects of their actual practice and application. It is not just that America's beginnings are, like all human endeavors, imperfect; it is that the liberating potential of their ideals is inextricable from the horror of the actual efforts to make them real. Yes, there is courage and nobility in John Winthrop's shipboard call to his fellow colonists to create in the new land the Gospel's "city on the hill," shinning its charity as an example to all the world. But, of course, colonial history is far from being a beacon of charity. As West puts it colorfully in an interview: "The paradisial city and all the other mess and lies and so on. I say no, no. America's a very fragile experiment predicated on the disposition of the lands of indigenous people and the enslavement of African people and the subjugation of workers and women and the marginalization of gays and lesbians."[10] There is something undeniably powerful in those revolutionary beginnings, but there is a blatant and blind brutality in that power as well.

A similar disconnect is present in America's founding documents. The ideas and rhetoric envisioning an all-embracing community of equals is impressive, but the words contradict themselves by failing to enfranchise women and acknowledge the full personhood of slaves. "These realities made many of the words of the Declaration of Independence ring a bit hollow."[11] It would not be difficult to identify such hypocritical schizophrenia throughout the course of American history, art, and life. It is not just that America has not lived up to its ideals. All societies have failed in that regard. But in America, it is precisely those things about which it feels its deepest pride, that are also the source of its darkest shame. It is this strange juxtaposition of pride and shame that, West argues, is distinctive to America. "We are exceptional because of our denial of the antidemocratic

---

10. West and Ritz, *Brother West*, 17.
11. West, *Race Matters*, 156–7.

foundation stones of American democracy. No other democratic nation revels so blatantly in such self-deceptive innocence, such self-paralyzing reluctance to confront the night-side of its own history."[12] What makes this hypocrisy so frustrating to West is the thoroughness with which it undercuts any meaningful democratic conversation about the need for change and the directions it might take. Many commentators have noted America's tendency to exceptionalism, to proclaiming that it is unique among nations, but West's paradoxical take on this tendency raises the sorts of questions that nudge to self-reflection.

Another of West's characteristics of American civilization is also a revealing contradiction between image and reality: the hybrid culture of many diverse people with a collective self-definition of homogenous Anglo-American culture. Few civilizations can match America's for the number and diversity of peoples involved in its formation. West identifies three broad groups: indigenous peoples, European migrants, and their African slaves.[13] He is well aware, of course, that each of these groups included a variety of subcultures within them. Europeans initially came from France, England and Spain. Indigenous peoples included Iroquois, Pequots, and Algonquin. African slaves included Igbo, Yoruba, and Kongo. Yet, despite its actual panoply of peoples and languages, America's self-image, its vision of beauty and value, is simplistically British. Given its pervasive verbal insistence on the equality of all people and the pervasive reality of its hybrid colors and customs, it is strange that America's national imaginary remains so stubbornly and purely white.

West explains this disconnect by arguing that the country's powerful elite needed to reduce its multiple diversity to a basic racial divide of black and white peoples. The fabrication of such a simplistic divide proved crucial to America's development as a "civilization." America's welcoming image as a classless beacon of opportunity for white European peoples was, West argues, inextricable from its degradation and exploitation of darker skins.

> What made America distinctly American for them [Irish, Italians, Poles, Welsh] was not simply the presence of unprecedented opportunities, but the struggle for seizing those opportunities in a new land in which black slavery and racial caste served as the floor upon which white class, ethnic and gender struggles could be diffused and diverted ... From 1776 to 1964—188 years of our

---

12. West, *Democracy Matters*, 41.
13. West and Ritz, *Brother West*, 17.

Section IV—Pragmatic Moments

218-year history—this racial divide would serve as a basic presupposition for the expansive functioning of American democracy.[14]

In other words, African Americans were not just one ethnic group among the many who made up America, albeit one that failed to become as well integrated into the dominant culture as, say, Irish Americans or Polish Americans had. Rather, African Americans functioned as the "Other" against whom the European and lighter-skinned ethnicities were unified into an American culture. The energy for "America's" expansion depended on the creation and maintenance of an "anti-" or "un" American group against whom progress could be measured

Ralph Ellison, in a famous essay for *Time Magazine* entitled "What America Would Be Like Without Blacks," asserted that "whatever else the true American is, he is also somehow black."[15] Ellison argued that so much of America culture—its music, sport and slang, for example—has been influenced by blacks that "most American whites are culturally part Negro American without even realizing it." West begins the introduction to *Race Matters* with Ellison's quotation about the "true American" being black, but then goes even further than Ellison in exploring the complicated way in which all Americans are "culturally part Negro." West suggests that it is not just that African Americans have injected many more positive things into the culture than is widely recognized; it is that, for much of its formation, America has used blackness as a negative definition of itself. Blackness becomes the very thing that America provides its citizens the opportunity to rise above. This negative definitional process explains why blacks have failed to become as integrated into American society as other groups. It also provides clues as to why, according to West, a nation so hybrid and indebted to blacks in blatantly obvious and foundational ways could be so lily white in its envisioning of itself, in its imaginary.

I have focused on two paradoxical qualities from one specific text in which West tries to characterize American culture, but similar insights and analyses can be found throughout his work. Some are meant mainly as Socratic prods for further reflection. For example, he labels America "the most death-denying of modern civilizations."[16] He is not trying to make an empirical claim here, that we spend more on anti-aging cosmetics, for example, than other nations. Instead, he is aiming for Socratic reflection. Is

---

14. West, *Race Matters*, 156–7.
15. Ellison, "What America Would Be Like Without Blacks."
16. West, "Afterword," 348.

there something strange, distinctive, in America's relationship with death? Certainly our medical system is structured to prolong biological life at all costs, without any concern for its quality. West puts the meaning of death at the heart of philosophy and insists, with Montaigne, that learning how to die is the most basic of philosophical tasks.[17] Whether or not America is actually "the most" death-denying of countries is debatable, but West's intent is to stimulate thinking on the varied and ingenious ways Americans devise to evade this philosophical topic.

Another characterization of American culture that West highlights throughout his work is the simplistic fervor of our capitalism. He notes that, at least in certain of its early colonies, "America is a company before it's a country."[18] Perhaps this is why we tend to identify human freedom itself with the freedom of production and consumption necessary to sustaining the economic system of capitalism. "Calculations and cost benefits hold sway in almost every sphere of U.S. society."[19] Certainly, a capitalistic environment is not peculiar to America, but it is uniquely championed here and permeates our life more extensively than in other countries. In America, not only does the market drive health care, education and politics more deeply than in other developed countries, but its citizens tend to take deep pride in that fact. West argues that America's confidence in the market as the most efficient and fair instrument of social organization and wealth distribution has become a fundamentalism as blindingly dangerous as any of its religious forms.[20] This "free-market fundamentalism" has been one of the major stumbling blocks in America's efforts to actualize democracy. The "corporate marketeers" have been especially effective in the moral education that surrounds day to day life. "The incessant media bombardment of images (of salacious bodies and mindless violence) on TV and in movies and music convinces many young people that the culture of gratification—a quest for insatiable pleasure, endless titillation, and sexual stimulation—is the only way of being human."[21] America's brand of capitalism is surely something distinctive about it.

Again, West does not intend these examples as a definitive account of American civilization. They merely demonstrate some of the diverse ways

17. West and Ritz, *Brother West*, 3.
18. West, *Hope on a Tightrope*, 45.
19. West, *Race Matters*, 26.
20. West, *Democracy Matters*, 3ff.
21. West, *Democracy Matters*, 135.

AMERICA AS AN ETHICAL CHOICE

he has worked to understand it, and some of his tentative and fallible conclusions. They exemplify not just perceptive cultural criticism, but concrete ways of reflecting on perennial issues in philosophy.

AMERICA AS AN ETHICAL CHOICE

In his preface to *Keeping Faith,* West asks himself the same sort of questions about his commitment to America that Socrates raised about his own commitment to Athens the night before his execution. West's wife, in 1993, is Ethiopian and he literally has a home and family in that country. In addition, as an African-American, his ancestral home is Africa and the history of his people's relocation to, and life in, America has been an exceptionally brutal one. Finally, he finds especially "depressing and debilitating" the fact that "race still so fundamentally matters in nearly every sphere of American life."[22] Unlike Socrates, West is not facing death, but he certainly has good reasons for leaving his country and committing to another.

Yet, like Socrates, West finds that the moral path, for him, lies in remaining here. He has no illusions about contemporary America. Its dream of real democracy is still deferred and, in some ways, the presidency of Obama has made it even more difficult to believe in because, as West has not failed to point out, Obama is as deeply tied to corporate money and market culture as was his Republican predecessor. Yet, West chooses not just to reside in American but to *be American*. "I try to muster all that is within me, including my rich African and American traditions, to keep faith in the struggle for human dignity and existential democracy."[23]

Why? What, precisely, is the object of the faith that West is keeping? What does he understand the moral meaning of America to be? What is being affirmed in embracing citizenship, in making a political commitment to the United States of America?

West entitles his introduction to *The Cornel West Reader,* "To Be Human, Modern and American." In that short essay he briefly explains his understanding of these three basic characteristics of who he is. His explanation of nationality begins as follows: "To be American is to be part of a dialogical and democratic operation that grapples with the challenge of being human in an open-ended and experimental manner."[24] In order to unpack

---

22. West, *Keeping Faith,* xv.
23. West, *Keeping Faith,* xvi.
24. West, *Cornel West Reader,* xviii.

the essential elements in this statement it is necessary to realize that, like a good preacher, West circles the same basic definition in an amazing variety of ways. I want to utilize some of those ways to emphasize three aspects essential to his understanding of America: that it is "dialogical" democracy and that this dialogue must be both "open-ended" and "experimental."

The first aspect of American democracy that needs emphasis is that it is "dialogical." West's vision of America is not so much people standing in line to vote as people in a circle animated by conversation; not a senator on the Congressional floor, but Socrates in the Athenian agora. The level of a society's democracy is not, in the final analysis, determined by the fairness of its election laws or by its constitutional structure, but by the quality of its conversation on the street. "[D]emocracy is more a verb than a noun."[25]

What Socrates discussed every day on the street, as he proudly testified at this trial, was virtue, that is, what the good life looks like for human beings and how it can best be achieved. Such communal, intellectual work is the necessary foundation for any meaningful political activity. The ultimate focus of democratic conversation is "the challenge of being human" both in its long term goals and its concrete social organization. West embraces this broad Socratic understanding of politics.

An essential aspect of this conversation is that it include voices from the past as well as the present. West usually begins his own essays and chapters with at least one quotation from someone else. Both his written work and his interviews are saturated with names and book titles. This "name dropping" is neither a display of his erudition nor a blind deference to history, but an insistence that effective dialogue include all voices, especially those who have shaped the current understanding of the issues under discussion. This, of course, includes minority voices and those who have been silenced in the past. And the voices are not to be limited to philosophers and politicians, but include all types of thinkers and artists. "The penetrating visions and inspiring truth-telling of Ralph Waldo Emerson, Walt Whitman, Herman Melville, Eugene O'Neill, W.E.B. Du Bois, James Baldwin, John Coltrane, Lorraine Hansberry, and Toni Morrison exemplify the profound potential of democracy in America."[26] This is just one of West's many lists of important American voices. It is not definitive, nor intended merely as an acknowledgement of his own personal influences; rather, it represents

---

25. West, *Democracy Matters*, 68.
26. West, *Democracy Matters*, 67.

his conviction that the past actively have a voice in any present political conversation.

Another crucial aspect of conversation in West's eyes concerns the participants presently engaged in it. If the conversation is to be an intellectually honest one, that is, one that involves rigorous self-questioning and transcends parochial prejudice, there needs to be not only universal access to the conversation, but universal involvement in it. "The ethical precondition for democracy is to allow every voice of the citizenry to be heard in the basic decisions that shape the destiny of its people."[27] West argues that any real commitment to democratic dialogue requires a kind of affirmative action, a special attention to the voices of the marginalized. This is not just a demand of justice, but a demand of rationality. West endorses Adorno's insistence that a condition of truth is to allow suffering to speak. It is precisely those who benefit least from the status quo, who are most likely to see where it is logically flawed. It is this concern for the marginalized that West admires in Socrates when he calls Meno's slave boy into their discussion about the nature of education.[28] Since the slave boy is the one with the least access to education, truth demands his presence in any genuine discussion about it.

West takes this democratic insistence on equality of voice one step further. "Is a multiracial and multisexual *political* democracy the best we [Americans]—or humankind—can do? Is economic democracy in a global economy a pipe dream?"[29] West suggests that, if one is serious about democracy as an activity in which all equally speak and are equally heard, then some form of economic equality seems logically necessary.

West frequently characterizes his thought as "prophetic" and connects the term's origins to "the Jewish invention of the prophetic commitment to justice—for all peoples."[30] He finds something philosophically important in Amos, Isaiah, and Jeremiah that he does not find in Socrates, and that is compassion. "[Socrates'] profound yet insufficient rationalism refuses to connect noble self-mastery to a heartfelt solidarity with the agony and anguish of oppressed peoples."[31] Because of this, Athenian democracy is incomplete and needs Jerusalem. American democracy must be fed by

---

27. Gates and West, *African-American Century*, xiii.
28. West, *Democracy Matters*, 17.
29. West, *Cornel West Reader*, xx.
30. West, *Democracy Matters*, 17.
31. West, *Democracy Matters*, 213.

streams from both great cities. But, West's argument that democratic conversation include some "preferential option for the poor," rests primarily not on a call for compassionate tears, but on what is logically needed for any robust and honest dialogue.

Once it is clear that democracy is not an organizational structure, a legal code, or a judicial system of enforcement, but the continuous discussion on which all of these must rest, West's constant reminder that America is an "experiment—precious yet precarious" becomes more understandable.[32] America is not a physical territory we inhabit or a citizenship whose legal papers we possess; it is a responsibility for conversation to which we are daily called. West's American is like Kierkegaard's Christian; one is always only becoming one. This also sheds light on why West understands his intellectual task as inherently a moral and prophetic one, as calling America back to its founding words and the job of enacting them.

The second aspect of West's definition of American dialogical democracy that needs emphasis is that it be "open-ended." Real conversation must include a certain type of intellectual humility. Dogmatism is utterly out of place. The modern thinker, according to West, is someone especially sensitive to the historicity of truth claims and the fallibility of human knowledge. This sensitivity does not result in any simplistic relativism or nihilistic paralysis, but it does make political conversation "risk ridden" and "dangerous,"[33] since nothing is above question and everything is on the table. The most un-American of activities is the confrontation of dogmas played out so often on the floor of Congress, the airways of talk radio and the platforms of social media.

The third aspect of dialogical democracy that needs emphasis is its "experimental manner." According to West, an experimental spirit has marked the best of American life and enterprise. From its early settlements onward, American society was founded on a willingness to try things out. We are not only convinced that things can always be better, we are ready to jump in and explore ways to make them so. The fact that we are willing "to downplay history in the name of hope, to ignore memory in the cause of possibility"[34] has often led to a rosy naiveté about the brutal evils in the world and in ourselves. Americans all too easily forget, for example, not just our genocidal dealings with indigenous peoples in the past, but the racial

---

32. West, *Cornel West Reader*, xviii.
33. West, *Cornel West Reader*, xvii.
34. West, *Cornel West Reader*, xvix.

disparities in our present prison industrial complex and the militaristic focus of our exports. However, America's raw energy has been undeniably inventive and has yielded, according to West, "forms of modern self-making and self-creating unprecedented in human history."[35] This frontier ethos has been evident not just in physical territories, including extraterrestrial space, but in our entrepreneurial embrace of capitalism and the extensive reach of our popular culture. West wants to see this experimental energy, this embrace of the untried, so present in various aspects of American life, pervade our political conversation about the kinds of lives that are good and the forms of community that might sustain them.

West argues that it is to the vitality of such democratic conversation that the choice of America commits one. This conversation must be fearlessly open and ongoing, it must actively involve the voices of all participants, and be especially supportive of ethical creativity. Such conversation, almost indistinguishable from the Socratic path of philosophy, is the fundamental meaning of America and, for West, the proper object of any pledge of allegiance made to it.

BLUES, JAZZ, AND DEMOCRATIC VOICE

Nietzsche realized early in his career that the key to unlocking the soul of Ancient Greece lay in understanding how it came to give birth to the art form we know as theater, as tragedy. In a similar vein, West's understanding of America is deeply intertwined with his experience of African American musical forms and his convictions about the role they have played in American life and culture. He includes in these musical forms: spirituals, blues, jazz, rhythm & blues, soul, and hip hop. He believes that blues and jazz are not only the most original art form America has created,[36] but also "the most American of art forms."[37] In other words, they are not only a uniquely new art form, but the art that is most characteristically American. He maintains that the entirety of "American musical heritage rests, in large part, on the artistic genius of black composers and performers."[38] He offers Louis Armstrong, Bessie Smith, Duke Ellington, Ma Rainy, John Coltrane, and Sarah Vaughan as some of the towering examples of this artistic ge-

35. West, *Cornel West Reader*, xviii.
36. West, *Democracy Matters*, 85.
37. West, *Democracy Matters*, 91.
38. West, *Hope on a Tightrope*, 116.

nius.³⁹ Since he frequently describes his own intellectual place in America as that of "a blues man in the world of ideas—a jazz man in the life of the mind,"⁴⁰ I want to clarify his understanding of those two musical forms because they throw light on his understanding of the meaning of America.

Blues and jazz are types of music that had their roots in African American communities of the Deep South at the start of the 20th century. In certain instances, they are quite distinct forms. Robert Johnson's *Cross Road Blues* for example, is obviously quite different from Duke Ellington's *Sophisticated Lady*. In many other instances, however, the two forms are hard to distinguish; they interconnect and overlap. Jazz artists like Louis Armstrong and Billie Holiday certainly "sing the blues," and bluesmen like Robert Johnson and Muddy Waters creatively improvise in their performance. What primarily identifies "the blues" for West is a certain sensibility about the world which he calls "tragicomic." This sensibility is not limited to musicians or African Americans. He calls Tennessee Williams, for example, "the great white literary bluesman."⁴¹ West identifies jazz, on the other hand, primarily with improvisational individuality, with finding one's own voice. Let me briefly explain his understanding of each.

West endorses and utilizes Ralph Ellison's famous definition of the blues as "an autobiographical chronicle of personal catastrophe expressed lyrically."⁴² West argues that the blues can only come from someone who has seen the darkest aspects of human behavior and not closed her eyes. Without turning away from the pain of life, for example, Billie Holiday has the skill to express what she sees and feels in some form of beauty, some song. Her spirit is not undone by the misery she intimately knows; she transcends it in the very act of singing it. "That is the essence of the blues: to stare painful truths in the face and persevere without cynicism or pessimism."⁴³ West values the blues not just for its aesthetic powers, but as an aid in avoiding any form of nihilism, either philosophical or existential, that undermines a spirit of hope.⁴⁴ This creative tension between knowing in one's bones the inherent limitations of human community, yet struggling mightily for change is what he terms "tragicomic hope." West argues that

39. West, *Democracy Matters*, 91.
40. West, *The Cornel West Reader*, xv.
41. West, *The Cornel West Reader*, 91.
42. West, "Strength in Blues," 3.
43. West, *Democracy Matters*, 21.
44. West, *Race Matters*, 17–24.

such hope is a profound ethical stance, one that is best exemplified in the life of Jesus Christ and the work of great artists like Shakespeare, Beethoven and Chekhov—and one he struggles to maintain in his own life. He believes that "the blues is the most profound interpretation of tragicomic hope" that America has so far created.[45]

Jazz, as a musical form, is notoriously difficult to define. West borrows Duke Ellington's definition, claiming simply that "jazz is freedom."[46] A jazz saxophonist like Charlie Parker, for example, is not interested in articulating a score's mandated progression of notes, but in forging his own path, in the individuated tonal color he can coax out of his instrument. As West says, "What is jazz all about? It's about finding your voice. It's about that long, difficult walk to freedom."[47] While a jazz singer like Sarah Vaughan is familiar with a wide variety of styles, she is never tied to any particular one. Ella Fitzgerald is not afraid to add notes or words or sounds (scat) to a familiar song and lets the intensity of the performance guide what is produced. The ability to improvise effectively implies a mastery and virtuosity of craft acquired only with rigid discipline. It also involves complicated levels of intellectual agility as the singer interacts with both her musicians and her audience. Democracy is, of course, only as strong as the individuals who make it up and jazz musicians are "eloquent connoisseurs of individuality in their improvisational arts and experimental lives."[48] Interestingly, West characterizes his own intellectual work as making "improvisational use of philosophical traditions."[49]

West sees blues and jazz not just as significant influences in musical history and art, but as significant influences on the American project of democracy in at least three ways. The first has to do with its honesty in approaching the darker aspects of life. We have noted already West's frustration with the American tendency to ignore the dark and tragic sides of life. He decries the "cheap optimism" and "innocent sentimentalism" that blinds many Americans.[50] "It's a very American thing, in some ways, to be sentimental, to create your own little world, live in your bubble."[51] This

---

45. West, "Strength in Blues," 3.
46. West, *Democracy Matters*, 91.
47. West, *Hope on a Tightrope*, 118.
48. West, *Democracy Matters*, 91.
49. West, "Afterward," 355.
50. West, *Democracy Matters*, 216.
51. West, "Strength in Blues," 3.

blindness seeps even into America's philosophers. While West values much in pragmatism's canon, especially Dewey, he argues that "Dewey failed to seriously meet the challenge posed by Lincoln—namely, defining the relation of democratic ways of thought and life to a profound sense of evil."[52] What West finds ethically valuable in the blues is that the truth of its profound sorrow does not shrivel the hopeful spirit of its performers. The blues "expresses righteous indignation with a smile and deep inner pain without bitterness or revenge."[53] In this it can be a tool enabling America to face its dark side honestly, without embittering its soul.

As we have seen, for West, "democracy is about voice lifting, and lack of democracy is about lack of voice."[54] But obviously, jazz is also very much about "voice lifting." This is a second way jazz adds to democratic conversation in America. Achieving a unique individuality in the face of the existential limitations confronting all human beings is a monumental task even under the most privileged of circumstances; it would seem nigh impossible under the dehumanizing conditions America imposed on its slaves. Yet, jazz and blues are proof not just that it can be done, but that it can be done with splendor. "I have always marveled at how such an unfree people as blacks in America . . . invented such odes to democratic individuality and community as in the blues and jazz."[55] As noted previously, the conversation that West identifies with democracy does not happen primarily in the halls of legislatures or the pages of the *New York Times*, but on the airways and in the streets. Blues and jazz are vibrant models of voice raising and that is the bedrock of any genuine democracy.

West argues that music was not only "the first major cultural point of contact between whites and blacks," but the first incontrovertible evidence for average white Americans that blacks had profound cultural depths and were, in aesthetic sensitivity, equal to themselves.[56] "[Whites] affirmed our cultural excellence based on the quality of the music and style."[57] The cultural respect blacks gained in the musical arts paved the way for other forms of respect. Certainly, there would be difficult and bloody political work needed in the civil rights struggles of the 60's, but jazz and blues laid

52. West, *Cornel West Reader*, 175.
53. West, *Democracy Matters*, 19.
54. West, *Hope on a Tightrope*, 120.
55. West, *Democracy Matters*, 216.
56. West, *Democracy Matters*, 92.
57. West, *Hope on a Tightrope*, 115.

important groundwork for these struggles. West sees a similar liberating dynamic operative in hip hop music today,[58] although he has been critical of its misogynistic and homophobic elements.

That these musical forms are an "ode to community" is the third way they serve democracy. Historically, music was a means of establishing communication and community among the enslaved peoples because they did not always share a common verbal language.[59] For West, music is a communal force deeper than language, beyond language. Likewise, the improvisational nature of jazz requires an exceptional level of communal give and take among the performers. It is very much "about being in a group with antagonistic cooperation, which means bouncing against one another so that you're giving each other more and more courage to engage in higher levels of collective performance."[60] Traditional orchestral music requires a strong central conductor for its effective performance; jazz, on the other hand, works best as a mutually attuned democracy. It should be noted that West's own intellectual work has been far more collaborative than most of his colleagues in the humanities and has crossed several disciplinary boundaries

It is a truism of jazz and blues that they blend elements of African music like polyrhythms and expressive vocality with European forms and instruments. Such blending requires a creative and ongoing dialogue. The strength of a democracy, according to West, is dependent upon the extent to which those on the margins are actual participants in the conversation that shapes the social life of the community. In other words, the task of a democratic citizen is not only to find a voice, but to make it heard. West demonstrates that African American music is not just a form of entertainment, "not simply a music to titillate,"[61] but a serious counter-cultural voice in America's efforts at democratic conversation.

> The blues professes to the deep psychic and material pains inflicted on black people within the sphere of a mythological American land of opportunity. The central role of the human voice in this heritage reflects the commitment to the value of the individual and of speaking up about ugly truths: it asserts the necessity of robust dialogue—of people needing to listen up—in the face of

---

58. West, *Democracy Matters*, 92.
59. West, *Hope on a Tightrope*, 110.
60. West, *Hope on a Tightrope*, 118.
61. West, *Democracy Matters*, 20.

entrenched dogma . . . The stress the blues placed on dialogue, resistance, and hope is the very lifeblood for a vital democratic citizenry.[62]

Although West is referring specifically to the blues here, the ideas apply equally to both musical forms.

If America is to come anywhere near "achieving our country,"[63] the peoples on whose backs its economic and territorial growth was built, must have an active and equal voice in the conversation that constitutes its democracy. Blues and jazz are historical examples of forms that voice has taken. Their content, structure, and style offer lessons particularly needed in the corporate and class dominated workings of contemporary America. In addition, they have been crucial sources of energy and spirit for an oppressed people in dark times and might fulfill a similar function for a wider America in its present struggles for democracy. Far from being the "white man's burden," West wonders "whether American democracy can survive without learning from the often-untapped democratic energies and lessons of black Americans."[64]

CONCLUSION

Cornel West's intellectual work does not fit neatly into the usual academic categories. He has a PhD in Philosophy from Princeton and is presently Professor of Philosophy and Christian Practice at Union Theological Seminary, but in the course of his career he has held academic appointments in Religion (Princeton), American Studies (Yale Divinity School), and African-American Studies (Harvard) among others. However one categorizes his work, it centers, as he himself repeatedly attests, on the meaning of America. West insists that, even in a global world, nationality is an inescapable source of identity and crucial to any self-understanding worthy of the name. It is also a topic inherent in any conversation about what community involves in the 21st Century and about what kinds of public communities are desirable in a global world.

---

62. West, *Democracy Matters*, 93.

63. The phrase refers to James Baldwin's call at the end of his essay, "The Fire Next Time," to "end the racial nightmare" (Baldwin, *Fire Next Time,* 141). West uses the quotation to open *Race Matters.*

64. ˆWest, *Democracy Matters,* 216.

Section IV—Pragmatic Moments

West's performance of his intellectual work, as he again repeatedly attests, is deeply Socratic in its roots and vision. Like Socrates, West's desire to 'know himself' is paramount and includes both his personal self, struggling with the inevitability of death,[65] and his social self, struggling with the enactment of American democracy.[66] Like Socrates, he cannot separate his own philosophical quest from the task of calling others to self-reflection and self-knowledge.

> I've got to forge a unique style and voice that expresses my own quest for truth and love. . . . I must break through isolated academic frameworks while, at the same time, I must build on the best of academic knowledge. I must fuel the fire of my soul, so my intellectual blues can set others on fire.[67]

Undeniably, West's intellectual practice is not that of the typical professor in American universities today, but it does seem quite close, especially in its dialogical and aural forms, to that of Socrates.

Although Cornel West's philosophy and modes of philosophizing have developed and changed over the years, I would agree with Rosemary Cowan that his basic goals and methodology have remained remarkably consistent.[68] From the very beginning, one of his goals has been to develop a critical understanding of America, of its underlying meanings. What I have tried to do in this paper is provide definite content to this understanding and explore some of the ways it has been articulated. First, I examined some specific ways that West finds the institutions and attitudes of American civilization distinctive. I then summarized his understanding of what American citizenship means ethically, the baseline commitments inherent in its founding vision. Finally, I explored the significance West gives to blues and jazz in American life. Since they are America's most distinctive artistic expression, they have played an important role in expressing its spirit and energizing its democracy.

The overall understanding of America that emerges from West's prodigious and multifaceted work is conceptually rich and stimulating. Inherent in this understanding is an ethical call to continuous dialogue about America and its meanings. The unconventional and creative forms his thinking has taken are consistent with his struggle to involve all in this

---

65. West, *Cornel West Reader,* xvi.
66. West, *Cornel West Reader,* xviii-xx.
67. West and Ritz, *Brother West,* 5.
68. Cowan, *Cornel West,* 172–3.

dialogue. Since his intellectual project seeks to enact this dialogue both in academic journals and popular media, it is to his credit that it seems to be happening in both places.

BIBLIOGRAPHY

Appiah, Kwame Anthony. *Cosmopolitanism*. New York: W. W. Norton, 2006.
Baldwin, James. *The Fire Next Time*. New York: Dell, 1964.
Cowan, Rosemary. *Cornel West: The Politics of Redemption*. Malden, MA: Polity, 2003.
Ellison, Ralph. "What America Would Be Like Without Blacks." *Time Magazine* (April 6, 1970). http://teachingamericanhistory.org/library/document/what-america-would-be-like-without-blacks/.
Gates, Henry Louis, Jr., and Cornel West. *The African-American Century*. New York: Simon & Schuster, 2000.
Steve Jones. "Cornel West's 'Never Forget' Aims to Shift Hip-Hop's Focus." *USA Today* (August 28, 2007). https://usatoday30.usatoday.com/life/music/news/2007-08-27-cornel-west-album_N.htm.
Nussbaum, Martha. "Liberal Education and Global Community." *Liberal Education* 90 (2004) 42–47.
Taylor, Astra, ed. *Examined Life: Excursions with Contemporary Thinkers*. New York: New Press, 2009.
Unger, Roberto Mangabeira, and Cornel West. *The Future of American Progressivism*. Boston: Beacon, 1998.
West, Cornel, and David Ritz. *Brother West: Loving and Living Out Loud: A Memoir*. Carlsbad, CA: Smileybooks, 2009.
West, Cornel. "Afterword: Philosophy and the Funk of Life." In *Cornel West: A Critical Reader*, edited by George Yancy, 346–62. Malden, MA: Blackwell, 2001.
———. *The American Evasion of Philosophy*. Madison, WI: University of Wisconsin Press, 1989.
———. "Cornel West Flunks the President." *The New York Times Magazine* (July 24, 2011). https://www.nytimes.com/2011/07/24/magazine/talk-cornel-west.html.
———. *Cornel West Reader*. New York: Basic Civitas, 1999.
———. *Democracy Matters*. New York: Penguin, 2004.
———. *Hope on a Tightrope*. Carlsbad, CA: Smileybooks, 2008.
———. *Keeping Faith*. New York: Routledge, 1993.
———. *Race Matters*. New York: Vintage, 1994.
———. "Strength in Blues." *The Monarch Review* 14 (2012) 12.
Yancy, George. "Cornel West: the Vanguard of Existential and Democratic Hope." In *Cornel West: A Critical Reader*, edited by George Yancy, 1–16. Malden, MA: Blackwell, 2001.

Doing *Just* Philosophy:
On Cornel West, Love, and the Power of Public Discourse

Marsha Thrall

What does it mean to be human? Modern? American? In the introduction to the *Cornel West Reader*, Cornel West asks these questions in an attempt also to clarify what it means to be a public philosopher and theologian within a cultural landscape that often dismisses the value of active, public discourse.[1] Within the social structure of the United States, doing philosophy, particularly philosophy that focuses upon the discursive, public nature that is required in the personal practice of an ethic of love, imposes upon the philosopher a mandate to commodify their work; that is, in order to thrive in a manner that is acceptable within a monetized, quasi-democracy, philosophers must often manipulate their work in order to present work in a manner that is considered quantitatively valuable, rather than relying upon the qualitative nature of philosophical labor. West argues that such commodification and monetization is the result of a socio-cultural naïveté focused upon the tenuous hope of an eschatological moment that will allow the United States and its inhabitants to realize an illusive greatness that ignores the shameful violence and exploitation that this nation was built upon.[2] This paper will examine and question both West's attempt to pro-

1. West, "Introduction," xvi.

2. In the introduction to *The Cornel West Reader*, West questions whether America, "the last grand empire of the twentieth-century" can meet the challenge of "multiracial and multisexual political democracy," while also questioning whether or not democracy

vide a philosophical platform upon which public discourse can reside, as well as West's suggestion that being human requires both embracing and performing an ethic of love.

WHAT DOES IT MEAN TO BE AMERICAN?

In answering this question, West suggests that to be *American*, is to "be part of a dialogical and democratic operation that grapples with the challenge of being human in an open-ended and experimental manner."[3] And this humanness exists within a social structure that basically actively ignores the past, and all of the damage the past has wreaked upon the social landscape upon which "Americans" dwell. This damage, both blatant and collateral, has shaped an Americanized culture about which many are ignorant. This ignorance includes intentionally turning a blind eye to a historical narrative that tells the tale of a nation built upon the back of black and brown bodies stolen from their home continent and of humanity diminished for the comfort of white power structures. This ignorance includes ignoring a past in which this nation was populated by Western Europeans diminished to a lesser class, simply to allow original settlers and their descendants an illusion of continental purity. This ignorance sweeps away a past in which those native to this land were robbed and exterminated in mass acts of genocide while those who were left behind were colonized to reservations and force-fed whiteness as an act of dominance. This ignorance looks past a history when women were considered un-human, when being a woman meant subjection to body policing and abuse. West would argue that by ignoring this "past," Americans exist dualistically within a present that conveniently forgets a corrupted social inheritance in order to naively look forward to an unrealistic future bound in misunderstandings of hope, while living as unrepentant, individualistic replicates of our ancestors, within the present.

There is legitimization within West's arguments, and this legitimization has become manifest within the current political climate of the United States. This current political climate is one where the Empire has become a dominating and colonizing force against its very own population, with cries of "black lives matter" negated with retorts of "all lives matter." The

---

can, in reality, be a legitimate way of "being" within the world. This question is particularly compelling when posed along with the questions of what it means to be "human, modern, and American." See West, "Introduction," xx.

3. West, "Introduction," xvii.

Section IV—Pragmatic Moments

opportunity for refugees to seek asylum within the United States is met with criminalization simply because of religious misunderstanding. And women are given just enough illusion of freedom to be blinded to the ways in which this America's quasi-theocracy seeks to police the feminine body. Each and every symptom of the ills of inequity listed above are seen, by some, as the cure that will lead to "America" being great again. In our current political situation, it would seem that West's voice has been prophetic; that is, West's voice works to proclaim the ills, immaturity, and hubris that systematically infects and inscribes itself upon a cultural landscape too ignorant to remember the past, too bound to it's quasi-theocracy to acknowledge suffering and inequity in the present, and too hung up on the eschatological promise of "greatness" to hear the voices that are crying out to be heard and to see the bodies seeking to be counted within this confusing experiment with democracy.

However, West's utilization of the terms "America/American" makes me uncomfortable, beyond simply the cancerous terminology used as an inoculation, of sorts, of an "America" that has become too liberated for it's own good. West's assumption of the linguistic appropriation of the terminology of "America/American" creates a colonization, of sorts; a colonization through linguistic application that ignores regional borders of "America" that include Canadian and South American borders. In this ignorance, West lumps together the continental experiences of three separate places, in an attempt to create a linguistic short-hand that he intends to apply to the political culture of the United States, exclusively. And within this generalization, West fails to acknowledge the democratic maturity of Canada, while at the same time dismissing the ways in which the colonizing force of the United States has worked to further oppress and diminish the humanity of people who inhabit Americas that lie south of United States borders; thus complicating, and perhaps even negating his own critique of the United States by linguistically asserting that the entirety of the Americas are only as valid as measured against the flawed standards to which West holds the United States to account.

WHAT DOES IT MEAN TO BE MODERN?

Whether the sequence of questioning follows West's trajectory or my own, questioning personal philosophical practice as a modern acts as a fulcrum to examining the self through this examination of being human and doing philosophy. As such, West defines being modern as having the "courage to use one's critical intelligence to question and challenge the prevailing authorities, powers and hierarchies of the world . . . to be modern is to live dangerously and courageously in the face of relentless self-criticism and inescapable fallibilism; it is to give up the all-too-human quest for certainty and indubitability owing to the historicity of our claims."[4] Within his definition of being modern, West suggests that doing philosophy, as a Westian "modern" is to hold in tension the traditional tools of modernity; intellect, logic and reason with individual expressions of humanity—including, specifically, dialogue, art and music. West suggests that public applications of these expressions provide a framework in which the work of public discourse can begin as a subversive act, working towards the dismantling of the oppressive forces present within imperial foundations.

When examining the modern self, I believe there is value in acknowledging how doing philosophy as a personal, yet public practice of engaged discourse is an act of resistance in response to imperial domination and oppression. While the most recognized form of discourse takes shape as mediated conversation within a public setting, discourse can also take on life within acts of music, art, poetics and public demonstration, both the peaceful and the riotous kind. Discourse, itself, requires the courageous assertion and application of mind, body and voice as counter narrative to systems of domination and oppression. However, Empire often suggests that the submissive nature of polite, non-violent discourse is the standard to which power will accept echoes of dissension as a means of pacification. Sometimes, when voices have been systematically silenced, the only voice the courageous, philosophical, modern being is left with is the voice of anger, projected through the physical destruction of material, representative of the empire's oppression. In other words, to quote Martin Luther King, Jr., "a riot is the language of the unheard."[5] Therefore, being modern while doing philosophy requires the modernist to think critically and courageously, especially as it concerns not only the modernist's grasp

---

4. West, "Introduction," xvii.
5. King, "Address."

Section IV—Pragmatic Moments

of philosophy, but also keeping in tension the way that Empire subverts the critical mind, tricking some modern philosophers into believing that socially controlled, polite public discourse is itself liberation, in a culturally refined way. A virtuous, modern philosopher will not only examine how doing polite philosophy is crucial to examining their current social landscape, but will also examine how musical, artistic, linguistic, and yes, even violent expression are discursive tools that work to dismantle systems of oppression while allowing the individual to "be" in accordance with their individual humanity.

WHAT DOES IT MEAN TO BE HUMAN?

While West approaches the conversation of being "human" as a sort of preface to examining components of living that include being "American" and being "modern", it would actually seem that within the social structure that we exist in, examining humanity is a luxury permitted later within our lives, if, as a culture, "we" are allowed to examine our humanity at all. While West acknowledges that expressions of humanity manifest itself in many forms, including artistic, literary and musical expressions, he misses the mark in acknowledging that many people are categorized as commodities long before their ability to self-express is even made manifest within personhood. West seems to be working within in assumption that all who commit to examining life artistically, musically, or philosophically, have been afforded the opportunity to exercise these examinations always, and in meaningful and formative ways. In other words, West himself is operating from a place of privilege that he may not even realize is privilege; that is as a philosopher who was able to embrace and live within a philosophical life for the greater part of adulthood And it is within this living-out of a philosophical life that West's privilege is manifest within West's ability to live a life of personal truth. Because the nature of living within a capitalistic social structure often requires many to never realize their truth, West's place of living life as "a dramatist of philosophic notions"[6] is a place of privilege that most human beings will have limited ability to touch.

It is within the active living of one's truth, particularly as a philosopher, that an ethic of love becomes a means for the public philosopher to subvert the ways in which their truth, as it manifests within their work, is merely commodified—or presented for consumption within communities

6. West, "Introduction," xv.

of capitalism. And it is within this love ethic that being "human, modern, and American" manifests as something other than a civic existence within the Empire known as the United States. West points out that rather than simply produce music to be consumed and exchanged for economic currency, the human musician operating under an ethic of love creates artistic expression that is "profound music [that] leads us—beyond language—to the dark roots of our scream and the electrical heights of our silence."[7] The human intellectual, operating within an ethic of love is often able to produce written work that is "preeminently existential." And the philosophical, Westian modern has "the courage to use one's critical intelligence to question and challenge the prevailing authorities, powers and hierarchies of the world." As West explains it, operating under an ethic of love requires the musician, the intellectual, and the philosopher to examine life (individual and communal) through a lens that lays bare human condition, while using creative gifts to feed knowledge of this bare-ness to the remainder of community.

When privilege allows, the ability to examine what "being human" means, especially within a social setting that is structured to exploit humanity, is an integral exercise in liberation. Being able to recognize humanity is an eye-opening experience, leading to the ability to see the humanity of others. Acknowledging this "othered" humanity is often, at the least, uncomfortable but most times painful. Especially when our personal contributions to this suffering of the other are exposed in all of their exploitative forms. It is within these awakenings of humanity that visible expressions of hope are made manifest; within the public groanings of art and music lovingly shared within culture by the ancestors of the brown and black bodies that involuntarily laid the physical foundations for the society in which we live. It is within the hearts and souls of women who choose to give, listen, and love, despite being victims of past abuse and exploitation. It is within the bodies and minds of educators, descended from immigrants, who choose to dedicate their lives to educating and helping others discover and explore the humanity buried within bodies produced to be capitalized upon. Being human requires the human person to commit to an ethic of love; a love that isn't identified by the way our bodies chemically react to the other, but rather, a love that compels the self-examined human to break down barriers that prevent others from knowing their humanity is valuable.

---

7. West, "Introduction," xvii.

Section IV—Pragmatic Moments

CONCLUSION

In the spring of 2008, I was in my second semester of part time coursework at Mount Mary, and it was within this semester that I took "Search for Meaning." At the time, I was a practicing evangelical Christian who believed in biblical inerrancy and that questioning God was an act of sin against God, himself. And this piece is important, because it is often within this brand of Christianity that humanity itself is, at best, hidden behind a veil of our subordination to divinity, but at worst, considered abominable, sinful, dirty and ultimately unworthy of the Grace and Love given to us, by God as a sort of charitable act. Often, in some evangelical circles, we aren't allowed to love ourselves, because in loving self, we take our "eyes away from God." And it is within these spaces that it is nearly impossible to seek the wisdom necessary to discover the hope, joy and suffering that is a key component in working towards understanding what it means to be human.

It was in this semester, through the work assigned by Dr. Conlon, that the religious lenses through which I viewed the world were cracked, just a little bit. In reading works like Plato's Allegory of the Cave, the *Book of Job* (from a source outside of the biblical canon), and Descartes' *Meditations on First Philosophy*, particularly the third meditation, I started the journey towards both being hungry for work that exposed how other human beings grappled with this very human condition, but also towards beginning the work necessary to realize my own humanity. And it was within this space that I was introduced to the work of Cornel West, particularly the introduction to *The Cornel West Reader*. At the time, I struggled with West. He uses big words. He asks complicated questions that seem rhetorical, in that he already knows the answer he is looking for, but those answers aren't so clear to the casual reader. But most importantly, West challenges conventional notions of what it means to be Christian, to be human, and to practice a love ethic. Since this "Search for Meaning" experience, that feels like almost a lifetime ago, I have engaged West as a conversation partner, at least so far as his canon of work extends, and within these metaphorical, personal conversations, I have come to understand that following Jesus requires shaking off conventional Christianity, that I must shake off this conventionality in order to be the human that God created me to be, and in return for the gift of my humanity, I must actively work within the world as if the tenets of a love ethic were tattooed upon my soul by God's self. In other words, in order to be a biblicist, theologian and ethicist, I must reject the dogma that is related to conventional religion, and instead work to understand how

God is manifest both within myself and within the humanity of those who I share space with. Public discourse is key to living within a democratic ethic of love.

In closing, I want to thank Jim Conlon for dedicating his humanity to helping us, helping women like me, women who have been mistreated, abused and even commodified, to discover what it means to be human. Thank you for embodying a love ethic. We are grateful.

BIBLIOGRAPHY

King, Martin Luther, Jr. "Address to the Grosse Pointe Historical Society." http://www.gphistoical.org/mlk/mlkspeech/.

West, Cornel. "Introduction." In *The Cornel West Reader*. New York: Basic Civitas, 1999.

SECTION V

Temporal Moments: Teaching in Time

Before Sunset and the Truth of Time
JAMES CONLON

I'VE BEEN AT MOUNT Mary University a long time. So, it seems fitting that my "retirement" paper be about time, about a specific kind of experience of time and about the truth of time.

I'm going to begin by sharing with you the first scene from Richard Linklater's film, *Before Sunset* (2004), but I need to do a bit of groundwork to set the scene up. In an earlier Linklater film, *Before Sunrise (1995)*, an American student, Jesse (Ethan Hawke), meets a French girl, Celine (Julie Delpy), on a train in Europe. They meet when Celine changes seats to avoid a married couple arguing loudly, and both are surprised by the level of conversation they are able to achieve in a short amount of time. Jesse has to get off the train in Vienna to catch a plane back to America in the morning. He convinces Celine to get off the train with him and spend the night together talking and exploring the city. Although they clearly are attracted to each other, they are skeptical both of romance in general and the stereotype of the American-boy-meets-French-girl-in-Europe scenario in particular. When it comes time to part in the morning, they feel they have made an especially intimate connection, but distrust their feelings—given that they have known each other less than 24 hours. They hurriedly decide on a way to determine if their feelings have any truth. Since they have never shared last names, addresses or phone numbers, they have no way of contacting each other. This anonymity will give them time to put their experience in proper perspective. If, after six months of living and reflection, each feels as strongly about the other as they do now, they will meet again at the train station in Vienna. The movie ends as Celine's train pulls away and the audience is left wondering what actually happens in six months. Do they meet again? Should they meet again? It is a wonderful film, full of

Section V—Temporal Moments: Teaching in Time

good philosophical dialogue and I have had much fun exploring it in the classroom.

Nine years after *Before Sunrise,* Linklater made a sequel to it, *Before Sunset.* The sequel includes the same actors and is set nine years after Jesse and Celine parted in Vienna. As viewers of the sequel find out, the two never reunited as planned, nor have they been able to contact each other since they parted. However, Jesse has written a novel called, *This Time,* which is based on their meeting. He is now in Paris to promote the novel and is answering questions on it in a small bookstore. Unbeknownst to him, Celine is in the audience. Here's a bit of the scene.

Scene I—Shakespeare & Co. Bookstore

(We see the outside of the bookstore, then two signs: the first, a printed sign that reads "New Release, Jesse Wallace, *This Time*"; the second reads "Today, In Store Appearance, Author Jesse Wallace, Reading & Q & A, 5:30 P.M." Inside, Jesse is sitting at a table with copies of his book lying in front of him. Several reporters sit opposite Jesse. The bookstore owner sits to Jesse's right.)

Female reporter: Do you consider the book to be autobiographical?

Jesse: Hmmm . . . well, I mean, isn't everything autobiographical? I mean, we all see the world through our own tiny keyhole, right? I mean, I always think of Thomas Wolfe, you know, have you ever seen that little one page note to reader in the front of "Look Homeward, Angel," right, you know what I'm talking about? Anyway, he says that we are the sum of all the moments of our lives, and that, uh, anybody who sits down to write is gonna use the clay of their own life, that you can't avoid that. So when I look at my own life, you know, I have to admit, right . . . that I've . . . I've never been around a bunch of, a bunch of guns, or violence. You know, not really. No political intrigue or, uh, helicopter crash, right? (Nods at the bookstore owner, who nods back.)

But my life, from my own point of view, has been full of drama, right? And, uh, so I thought that if I could write a book that . . . that could capture** what it's like to really meet somebody. I mean one of the most exciting things that's ever happened to me is to really meet somebody, make that connection, and if I could . . . make that valuable,** you know, to capture that, that would be the attempt or . . . Did I answer your question?

. . .

Bookstore owner: We just have the time for one last question.

Male reporter: What is, uh, your next book?

Jesse: Ah . . . I don't know, man, I don't know . . . I've been . . . I've been thinking about this . . . Well, I always kind of wanted to write a book that all took place within the space of a pop song, you know, like 3 or 4 minutes long, the whole thing.

The story, the idea is that . . . there's this guy. Right? And . . . he's totally depressed. I mean, his great dream was to be a lover, an adventurer, you know, riding motorcycles through South America, and instead he's sitting at a marble table, eating lobster, and he's got a good job and a beautiful wife, right? But you know, everything that he needs. But that doesn't matter, 'cause what he wants is to fight for meaning.

You know, happiness is in the doing, right, not in the . . . getting what you want. So, he's sitting there, and just at that second, his little five year old daughter hops up on the table. And he knows that she should get down 'cause she could get hurt, but she's dancing** to this pop song, in a summer dress. And he looks down, and all of a sudden, uh, he is sixteen. And . . . his high school sweetheart is dropping him off, at home. And they've just lost their virginity, and she loves him, and the same song is playing on the car radio, and she climbs up and starts dancing on the roof of the car. And now, now he's worried about her! And she's beautiful, with a . . . a facial expression just like his daughter's.** In fact, you know, maybe that's why he even likes her. You see, he knows he's not remembering this dance, he's there. He's there in both moments simultaneously. And just like for an instance (Jesse snaps his fingers), all his life is just folding in on itself and it's obvious to him that time is a lie . . . (Jesse motions to his right, and is surprised and flustered to see Celine standing against the wall, listening to him) uh . . . that's it's all happening all the time and inside every moment is another moment, all . . . You know, happening simultaneously.

And, anyway, that's . . . that's kind of the idea . . . anyway.

Bookstore owner: Well, our author has to be going to the airport soon, so thank you all very much for coming here this afternoon. And a special thanks to Mr. Wallace for being with us. (Claps, and others join in clapping.) We hope to see you here again for your next book.[1]

**(These sections of dialogue are set against brief sequences of shots from Before Sunrise highlighting relevant moments of Jesse and Celine's experience in Vienna nine years before.)

---

1. Linklater, *Before Sunset*.

Section V—Temporal Moments: Teaching in Time

To analyze this wonderfully complex scene, let me begin with the experience of time Jesse is planning to make the centerpiece of his next novel. A thirty-ish man in the midst of a meaning crisis watches his five year old daughter jump up on a table and start dancing to a pop song. His daughter shouldn't be on the table; it's against the rules and it's dangerous. But it's summer and she's so beautiful. Watching his daughter, the man starts to remember his sixteen-year-old girlfriend dancing to the exact same song years ago. However, she is dancing on the roof of a car the night they lost their virginity. Suddenly the man realizes his daughter and his girlfriend are not just dancing to the same song, they have the same expression on their faces, the exact same innocence in their smiles. "Maybe," Jesse suggests, "maybe that's why he even likes her." To me, this suggestion is especially intriguing philosophically. In the man's experience of time, it has to be the girlfriend's face that comes first, right? He knew the girlfriend before his daughter existed. But Jesse is suggesting that it is the daughter's face that was the source of the man's attraction to his girlfriend. The man "knows he is not *remembering* this dance, he's there. He's there in both moments simultaneously. And just like for an instance all his life is just folding in on itself and it's obvious to him that time is a lie."

The simultaneity that Jesse is describing here happens when two moments, separated by years in time, are occurring side-by-side in our consciousness. While I don't believe this kind of simultaneity is an everyday occurrence, I suspect it is one that most of us have had in some form or other at some time in our lives. This kind of experience can disrupt our sense of causality. The man's feelings for his daughter seem to be causing the feelings for his girlfriend. Yet, the girlfriend came first in his experience of time. The feelings for his daughter dancing on the table are part of the "memory" of his girlfriend dancing on the car roof. In these kind of simultaneous moments, something doesn't seem right. Time seems to be a lie.

It is part of Linklater's genius that, right as Jesse is asserting that time is a lie, he sees Celine standing in the aisle of the bookstore and becomes quite flustered. The years between his two sightings of her, between seeing her board the train nine years ago and seeing her now in the bookstore, seem unreal, maybe even false. There does not seem nine years of distance between the two Celines he is experiencing. In short, Jesse is himself having in the bookstore the exact same simultaneity of moments he was just projecting for his novel.

But this collapse of time is not just happening to the characters in the film, it is happening to the actors as well. Hawke and Delpy are not just made up to appear nine years older, they actually are nine years older. Undoubtedly, much has happened in their lives since the earlier film. This was equally true for many of the viewers, including me, who saw *Before Sunset* when it first came out in 2004. It had been nine years since I saw the previous film and I had lived much life since then. But as I watched *Before Sunset* in 2004, I was remembering who I saw *Before Sunrise* with in 1995 and in what theater. I was remembering, too, the debates I had with students about whether Jesse and Celine actually did meet up in Vienna six months later. All my memories surrounding *Before Sunrise* were collapsing into my experience of watching *Before Sunset*.

To complicate the experience of viewing *Before Sunset* even further, it must be noted that nine years after making it, Linklater made a third film with the same characters and actors, *Before Midnight* (2013). I would claim that the future film, even though it existed only as a gleam in Linklater's' eye when he made *Before Sunset*, was part of my viewing experience of it in 2004. In other words, not only the previous film, but my imagined future film, was collapsing in on me as I watched *Before Sunset*. I think this collapse of time happened not just to me in 2004, but happens to viewers watching any of Linklater's three (so far) *Before* films now. Viewers experience in their own psyches the same simultaneity of moments that Jesse claims gives the lie to time.

****

The notion that time is a lie is certainly not original to Jesse. It has deep philosophical roots, and I want to tap into one of its most famous proponents, and that is Plato, specifically, in his *Symposium*. In the development of that dialogue, Plato utilizes the same kind of collapse of time that Linklater highlights in *Before Sunset*. The *Symposium* is Plato's account of a drinking party at which Socrates and others give speeches on love. But Plato opens the dialogue in a weird way. Rather than just beginning with a narrative of the party, Plato has a devotee of Socrates, Apollodorus, (who was not even at the party), recount its events in response to a question from a friend. Plato complicates Apollodorus' narrative even further by having him inform the friend that he had told the story of the party to Glaucon the day before. Strangely, however, when Glaucon had asked about the party, he was under the mistaken impression it was a recent event, when actually

Section V—Temporal Moments: Teaching in Time

it happened years earlier. Much has been written about why Plato provides such a convoluted preface to the *Symposium*. I would suggest that, right from the beginning, he wants to shake our confidence in the truth of time.

In addition to this weird preface, the *Symposium's* two climatic speeches about love, that of Socrates and that of Alcibiades, both rely on the kind of simultaneity of past and present moments that Linklater is exploring in *Before Sunset*. Socrates insists that his own speech is merely a repeat of a lesson about love that the priestess, Diotima, had given him years before. Her lesson from the past and Socrates' vibrant re-enactment of it at the drinking party, fuse those two moments of time together in the reader's consciousness.

Alcibiades's speech, too, is founded on a simultaneity of past and present moments. I have often wondered how a gifted director might film Alcibiades' drunken entrance into the party. Alcibiades is looking for the beautiful young host, Agathon, in order to commend him on his prizewinning play. He stumbles around the tables a bit and finally plops down beside Agathon on a couch. In his drunkenness, he does not notice who is sitting beside Agathon. I picture Alcibiades's eventual recognition that Socrates is also on the couch, to be similar in its fluster to Jesse's recognition of Celine in the Paris bookstore. As Alcibiades will soon confess to the assembled guests, he has shared a couch with Socrates once before. Years ago he had slyly maneuvered Socrates into sleeping over at his house and, hoping for a profession of love, had slipped into Socrates' bed and cuddled next to his naked body. Alcibiades' conflicted emotions that night years ago, his admiration of Socrates, his intense desire for him, and his rejection by him, become fused with his drunken present. The two different times with Socrates on the couch become indistinguishable as an experience and the duration between them seems arbitrary, a lie.

That lie, the false seductiveness of time, is at the heart of the speech on love that Socrates has given at the party. It is also, in a sense, the reason he did not respond to Alcibiades's embraces that cold night long ago when they first shared the same couch. For, as Diotima had taught him, love may begin with an attraction to one warm and beautiful body, but what love really desires is to move beyond those individualities and commune with timeless Beauty itself. For Socrates, the vibrant eternity of absolute Forms, of Beauty and Goodness, is the real truth. The more one is caught in a sequential chain of discrete moments, caught resisting the fusion of particulars into their conceptual essence, the less one abides in reality. Plato is definitely in agreement with Jesse that time is a lie. Eternity is the only truth.

****

But it is not just the ancients that have proclaimed time to be a lie. The theory of relativity is, in many ways, a contemporary variant of that claim. Einstein famously argues that time is not an irreversible, unidirectional flow, but a dimension of reality similar to the spatial. The past is misunderstood if it is viewed as a moment that once possessed existence and now is gone forever. Likewise, the future is misunderstood if it is viewed as a moment which has not yet come into existence. Rather, both past and future exist now, but as separate corners in a space-like matrix. According to Einstein, what humans experience as the durational flow between past and future is not intrinsic to time itself, but due to our limited, step-by-step method of getting from one corner of time to the next. The reason I cannot access the past or the future is not because they do not exist, but because I do not have the right travel equipment. I am wired to experience time in sequence, but sequence is not so much a truth about time, as a truth about me, about the limited kind of access to reality I possess.

When H. G. Wells wrote *The Time Machine* in 1895, the notion of time travel was purely the stuff of fiction. Now it is the stuff of physics. Jesse's claim that one can be in two moments simultaneously is no longer a metaphor. In Einstein's world, past, present and future exist simultaneously. Whether this simultaneity means time travel is a possibility for us and what happens to causality if it is, are questions being asked not just in novels, but in rigorous analytic philosophy. Perhaps it is not just in Jesse's fiction that a daughter's smile makes a man fall in love with her mother. In any case, Einstein provides interesting contemporary support for Jesse's contention that time is a lie.

****

Is it? Is time's sequencing of moments, its minute-by-minute plodding, actually an illusion? With the right equipment, the right contemplative attention, can we escape time's duration, step out of it and into the world of eternal ideas? Are Jesse, Plato and Einstein right?

I do not think so, nor does Linklater. However, to show why, I need to turn from the beginning of *Before Sunset*, to its ending. Jesse is scheduled to catch a plane back to his wife and son in America. Just as in *Before Sunrise*,

Section V—Temporal Moments: Teaching in Time

he and Celine have spent their short time together exploring the streets of each other's souls as well as those of the city they are in. Unlike the first film, however, Linklater makes the time of this film synchronous with the time of the action within it. In other words, the film takes the same time to watch as the characters have. This means the viewer is experiencing in the theater the same bite of minutes passing that Jesse and Celine are experiencing in Paris. In the course of eighty minutes, both characters have revealed a deep dissatisfaction with their present lives and the extent to which they have been haunted by their past intimacy in Vienna. Time's unfolding does not seem an illusion to them at all, but a relentless taskmaster, pushing them toward some decision about whether their romanticized memories can have anything to do with a realistic future.

Since Celine has read Jesse's fictional recreation of their meeting, he determines she must reciprocate by sharing some artistic creation of her own. So, with his assurance that he can still make his flight, she takes him to her apartment to play him one of her songs. The song is called "A Waltz for A Night," and it gently confirms that Vienna has figured as significantly in her dreams as it has in his.

After her song, Celine goes to the kitchen to pour some tea, and Jesse puts on a CD he finds on her shelf. It is Nina Simone singing the pop song "Just in Time." Celine, reminiscing about seeing Simone in concert, starts to echo the words of the song and imitate her body movements. Celine is, in effect, channeling Simone's performance just as Socrates channeled Diotima's lesson on love in the *Symposium*. *Before Sunset* began with Jesse envisioning a simultaneity of daughter and girlfriend dancing to the same song. Could that song have been "Just in Time," the very one Nina Simone/Celine is performing for us now? The film's beginning and its end are collapsing into each other.

At this point in my paper, if I were more tech savvy, I would have Nina Simone singing "Just in Time" as background to my words, but I'm going to have to rely on the old-fashioned method of quoting the lyrics to you, and you are going to have to imagine her classically trained fingers on the piano and her raspy voice melting around my words:

> Just in time, you found me just in time
> Before you came, my time was running low
> I was lost, the losing dice were tossed
> My bridges all were crossed, nowhere to go

If you do not know the song, or never heard Nina Simone sing it, pull it up on YouTube sometime. Hopefully, her singing will strengthen the philosophical argument I'm going to try to make.

> Now you're here and now I know just where I'm going
> No more doubt, no more fear, I've found my way
> *So, lets live today. Anyway. Change me. Change me.*
> *Change me, once again, and change my lonely life and lucky day.*
> (Simone's improvised version)[2]

There is no question that the song's lyrics and title fit perfectly with the film's romantic plot. As it is being sung, Jesse chooses to miss his plane and Celine gets what her own song wished for, "another try" with Jesse. In other words, as so often happens in the movies, they find each other just in the nick of time, just before their lives fade back into the passionless normality they have known since Vienna. But Linklater intends the song to do much more than just serve his plot. He intends it to be a philosophical response to Jesse's claim at the beginning of the movie that time is a lie. He wants to argue instead that the complex experiences of simultaneity that he explores in his movies, can happen "just in time," and only in time, nowhere else. If duration were truly a lie and the instantaneous presence of all moments the only reality, if moments were not sequenced one after the other, then—as the song proclaims—"I" would be lost; the individuality that is my unique consciousness could not happen. The human self is a performative entity that needs time to exist. Let me explain why.

What makes me an individual person is not that I am a distinctive substance to which outside events happen the way rain happens to a rock. Rather, these outside events happen self-consciously to me, that is, surrounded by my memories and my anticipations. My sensations of the world never happen to me purely in the present, they always come surrounded by pasts and futures of my choosing. For example, I never have just a simple, unalloyed sensation of a cloud in the sky; instead, like a film editor, I surround that present sensation with specific memories of previous clouds and specific worries about future weather. That choreographic arrangement of pasts and futures is my own distinctive stream of conscious experience, my self.

Imagine, as an even more specific example, Jesse's psychological editing process when he first sees Celine in the bookstore. It is not a simple

2. Styne et al., "Just in Time."

Section V—Temporal Moments: Teaching in Time

sensation of her colors and shapes. Inherent in that sight is his knowledge that she did not show up at the Vienna train station. For nine years he has concocted various answers for her absence. Each answer that he has given himself, along with the emotions evoked by it, has become intermingled with his original memory of her parting kiss on the train platform. This long chain of memories, and memories of memories, is now surrounding his sight of Celine. No wonder he becomes flustered and, much to her delight, starts to verbally stumble when he sees her. And, of course, he does not just have memories to contend with, all sorts of new hopes and fears are now going through his head. Will he tell her he made the expensive journey from the U.S. to Vienna? Will he reveal the depth of his heartbreak when she didn't show up? Will she explain why she wasn't there? What does he hope her explanation will be? What does he fear her explanation will be? Does he put the fear before the hope or the hope before the fear? And what does she hope for? Why is she in the bookstore anyway? The movie unfolds as an answer to these questions, but the point I want to make here is that the order in which Jesse fuses these memories and fears into his sight of Celine is, literally, who he is as a person. His present individual consciousness exists as a personalized editing of past and future moments. To exist as an individual self, it is not enough to have accumulated a particular string of happenings, I must be choreographing those happenings into a present stream of awareness. Each arrangement I create, like a montage of cinematic images, has its own individual meaning and makes me the person I am.

The engine for my arrangement, my dance of self-consciousness, is a future that I have not yet had access to. I need to have moments before me, in front of me, in order to motivate the editing process that creates my individualized awareness. Linklater's realization of this need for time is the genius of his three (so far) "Before" films. Their inherent durationality makes clear that if I was simultaneous with all the moments of my life, I would have no reasons to choose which past memories to fuse with my present sensations. I would have no ongoing stream of consciousness. I also need a future. I need to stand *before* a sunrise, or a sunset, or a midnight, *before* something, if I am to have a motivating energy for how to choreograph my ongoing awareness of present experience. I need to exist in the midst of unfolding time, not outside it.

In a timeless eternity, all my past and future moments would be like musical notes in one harmonized chord. They would all be there at once. Maybe it is possible for a divine consciousness to hear such a chord outside the stream of time, but it would be one consciousness, not many. Such an eternal chord might be exquisite in its own omniscient way, but there would be no multiplicity of individual consciousnesses happening within it. Those durational melodies would be lost in the sound of an eternal chord. For me to have "someplace to go," for my individual consciousness to be creatively happening, there needs to be that temporal sequencing of moments which in music is called melody and in metaphysics is called time. You can find the dance of individual consciousness "just in time" and only in time. If all moments existed simultaneously, if my bridges were all actually crossed and the die actually tossed, then the "I" that I am presently streaming would, indeed, be lost.

Before Sunset ends with Jesse's decision to miss his plane, and with Celine's collusion in that decision. In other words, it ends with their mutual choice to share a future, to be united in the sunset that is before them. They commit themselves to finding and re-finding each other in the dance of time, in time's movie. Jesse's contention that time is a lie, Plato's insistence that only eternity is real, Einstein's implication that duration is illusion, are mistaken. Time is not a lie, it is us. It is the movie we are seeing and the life we are immersed in. Precisely because we have a "before" in front of us, we can create the stream of consciousness that we are. Time is the only place a you and a me, in our individualized choreography of moments, can exist and find each other. "Just in time" can be sung just in time, not in eternity. This is the metaphysical meaning Linklater affirms at the end of *Before Sunset*. Our song, dance, dialogue, melody, movie, whatever you want to call this bittersweet stream that each of us is, is a durational performance that happens just in time. Linklater's movie glories in this, as does Nina Simone's music, as should we all.

BIBLIOGRAPHY

Linklater, Richard, dir. *Before Sunset*. 2004; US; Castle Rock Entertainment. Distributed by Warner Independent Pictures.
Styne, Jule, et al. "Just in Time." Performed by Nina Simone. https://www.youtube.com/watch?v=CgXUeRbel3c.

Just in Time
Considering the Moment in Teaching

Jennifer Hockenbery Dragseth

THE ETERNAL RETURN OF THE SAME

I HAVE BEEN TEACHING at Mount Mary University (formerly College) for over twenty years. This is still less than half of my colleague, Jim Conlon's forty three years. Since 1998, over 2000 students have passed through my classes. This is still less than half of Jim's 4000+ students. Yet, already there is a sense each semester of being caught in a Nietzschean eternal return of the same.

Friedrich Nietzsche's Zarathustra hypothesized, and the hypothesis initially made him gag as if being strangled by a serpent caught in his throat, that all things in time have already occurred infinitely many times and would continue to occur infinitely many more times. Nietzsche had read about this possibility in a physics journal, and it immediately struck him as an important philosophical and psychological thought experiment. What if every moment of one's life is lived exactly the same way in exactly the same order over and over for eternity? Nietzsche asked his reader to consider if the thought was terrifying or exhilarating. The answer, Nietzsche insisted, indicated the value of one's life in one's own value-making gaze.

In my mind, there is no need for a *gedanken* experiment. The eternal return of the same is part of the lived experience of the long-time teacher. I consider it each semester as the new students file into their seats for our required introductory course: *Search for Meaning*. Thirty women file into class. They are diverse enough from each other, perhaps, but not so different from the make-up of last semester's class. A few have taken a philosophy class before in high school or at a college from which they have transferred. No one remembers that philosophy means the love of wisdom but most know that philosophy has something to do with asking endless questions. They have heard of Socrates but know of none of the pre-Socratics. "Wait," someone asks, "I think I have heard of Sappho. Isn't she a lesbian?" The syllabus is explained, the rules of the course are given, the introductions are made. The sessions march forward chronologically. We read aloud Sappho's poems. We turn out the lights and re-imagine the Cave and a Light of truth that is brighter than cultural shadows. We quietly meditate with Lao Tzu, debate the role of obedience to political authority as encouraged by Confucius, and exegete a Gospel. There's a mid-semester break and suddenly the class finds itself in the 17th century discussing the possibility of algebra as a cure to Descartes' anxious worry that everything we experience may be part of a dream or worse a deception caused by an all powerful evil demon. The last weeks fly by, we race through the last four centuries. We pause to listen to Beauvoir's call to create freely a reality beyond the myths of femininity. We stumble on our way over Anzaldua's Spanish poetry and prose as we try to broaden our understanding of the permeability of the borderlands. Then we halt to prepare for exam week. In the final discussion hour, the students exclaim that they have learned much. They confess that they are in love with wisdom; they are critical questioners and creative thinkers. Their minds are more open, they say. For the rest of their lives they promise to be Socratic gadflies and midwives to their friends and family members and other teachers. The summit has been achieved. Deep breaths are taken. And then, after a teaching recess of several weeks, I find myself at the front of a classroom while thirty women file into the seminar room. No one knows that philosophy is the love of wisdom, but someone thinks she remembers that Sappho was a lesbian.

The life of a teacher would seem Sisyphean, except that the conscious center of my brain does not look down from eternity but is caught in time. This is a gift, of course. Each semester feels somewhat new. "I never thought of Descartes like that," I exclaim inwardly after a particularly good class discussion. "That joke I told today, now, that was funny." I compliment myself on staying fresh and current, until I find the folder from ten years ago—and the lecture notes that contain the same insight... and the same joke. Teaching undergraduate classes is like watching the same treasured film over and over. I think I am finding new things in it each time, because my consciousness is caught in the moment, unable to recollect the whole of my lived experience. I am laughing at Ethan Hawke's joke with Julie Delpy in *Before Sunrise* because I forgot the punchline yet again.

> "Vanity of vanities," says the Preacher;
> "Vanity of vanities, all is vanity...
> That which has been is what will be,
> That which is done is what will be done,
> And there is nothing new under the sun."[1]

CATCHING THE MOMENT

In graduate school I had a class on Aristotle's *Nicomachean Ethics* taught by the French Catholic philosopher Remi Brague who insisted that Aristotle had an important and practical message about time, eternity, and the moment. *Kairos*, the Greek demon of the moment, was depicted with his hair gathered in a pony tail notably tied at the forehead rather than the nape of the neck. As *Kairos* runs, the virtuous person has to be alert in order to grab *Kairos* and yank him by the pony tail in order to grasp the moment and seize the occasion. If the person is not paying attention, she will find herself looking at the back end of *Kairos*, unable to make use of the right time. Brague's French accent delighted us as he explained what this means in practical terms. "I was just in the faculty lounge having my lunch when I noticed that the Moment for class was just about to pass. My colleague told me not to worry, 'There is always time; the students will be with with us always.' But I knew I must run. For the Moment was at hand, if the clock's hand moved too far, the students would leave the classroom. And the Moment would be gone. Virtue is grabbing the Moment at the right time, in the right way, for the right reason. This Aristotle taught."

As a teaching assistant and then later as a young professor, Brague's Aristotelian image made me prepare thoroughly for class lectures. I always rushed to get there on time. I knew I must grab *Kairos* by the pony tail. I must seize the Moment and make the occasion of the class meaningful

---

1. Ecclesiastes 1:1, 9 (NIV).

for the student. But after a few semesters, most professors start to feel like Brague's colleague. There are always more students and more moments if we miss this one. If Sisyphus drops his rock today, he knows he will be able to roll it up the hill tomorrow just as well. In the span of a career, what is a moment? It will not matter if I take one more moment looking at emails in order to send one more idea into the cloud. A lazy kind of Platonism all too easily reigns as we consider this life, this class, as just a shadowy image of the Truth, a brief journey before eternity opens.

But Conlon's paper on *The Truth of Time* demonstrates something important about time and eternity. It is this: The Moment absolutely matters to us as we are temporal creatures. I think about Moments brought up by alumnae, Moments that shaped and changed their lives. One alumna cannot forget the evening on the rooftop garden in Rome drinking wine and talking about the philosophy of love with Conlon and her fellow philosophy students. Another alumna shrugged off her student loan debt saying the bank can't repossess the ideas in her mind, "Once I experienced that Moment in the classroom, the idea was mine forever." I have my Moments too. I remember sitting in the faculty lounge with Jim reading Kierkegaard, when he sighed after reading a passage in *Philosophical Fragments* and said, "That is so beautiful it has to be true." At that moment, reading a line about Christ sitting at the table with friends, while sitting at a table with a friend, I learned that it is in the Moment that new things do appear. It is not so much that we must grab and make use of *Kairos*, but that the Moment grabs us by the hair.

"But then my soul is filled with new wonder"[2]

THE TEACHER IN TIME

While the quotes in Jim's paper are from Plato and Linklater, I find that at least some of the ideas he puts forward about time are from Kierkegaard. Kierkegaard's pseudonym Johannes Climacus writes the *Philosophical Fragments* as an investigation of the paradox of the historical moment's relationship to eternal truths. More precisely, the text considers the role of the teacher in time. Climacus begins by considering the original philosophy teacher.

---

2. Kierkegaard, *Philosophical Fragments*, 44.

Section V—Temporal Moments: Teaching in Time

> Let us briefly consider Socrates, who was himself a teacher. He was born under such and such circumstances; he came under the formative influences of the people to which he belonged; and when upon reaching maturity he felt an impulse and call to this end, he began in his own way to teach others. . . . So understood, and this was indeed the Socratic understanding, the teacher stands in a reciprocal relation, in that life and its circumstances constitute an occasion for him to become a teacher, while he in turn gives occasion for others to learn something.[3]

Kierkegaard's Climacus considers Socrates to be the epitome of the best a human teacher can be. The human teacher, with humility, understands herself as an occasion for the students to seek understanding within themselves. The human teacher provides no actual new insight, but only an occasion. Through a process of dialogue, the student becomes aware of what she already knows eternally but has temporarily forgotten. Climacus explains, "Whoever understands Socrates best understands precisely that he owes him nothing, which is as Socrates would have it, and which it is beautiful to have been able to will[.]"[4]

But Climacus is struck with an idea, an idea that is not his own, an idea that is not remembered from eternity, but an idea that is new. The idea is transformative from the Moment it occurs to him in time. The possibility of such a new thing, of such an idea, of such a Moment, requires that he rethink his understanding of time and of teaching. In considering this, he writes,

> But if the entire situation is non-Socratic, as we have assumed, the disciple will owe *all* to the Teacher; . . .This relationship of owing all to the Teacher cannot be expressed in terms of romancing and trumpeting, but only in that happy passion we call Faith, whose object is the Paradox. But the Paradox unites the contradictories, and is the historical made eternal, and the Eternal made historical.[5]

Climacus is struggling to explain how teaching an eternal truth in time can occur. On one hand, the idea is eternal. On the other hand, the student's understanding of the idea is historical. She learns in time; she is changed in the Moment into a creature who understands the idea. This is a historical event.

---

3. Kierkegaard, *Philosophical Fragments*, 28.
4. Kierkegaard, *Philosophical Fragments*, 76.
5. Kierkegaard, *Philosophical Fragments*, 76.

Climacus worries that his text will be taken for "the most wretched piece of plagiarism."[6] Perhaps this is in part because the text of *Philosophical Fragments* seems to reference so directly Augustine's fourth century text *On the Teacher* which is a dialogue on the same theme that Climacus is tackling. In the dialogue, Augustine and his son Adeodatus are exploring how human words spoken by a human teacher to a human student are able to convey eternal Truths which transform the understanding of the student and often the teacher as well.

> Concerning universals of which we can have knowledge, we do not listen to anyone speaking and making sounds outside ourselves. We listen to Truth which presides over our minds within us, though of course we may be bidden to listen by someone using words. Our real Teacher is the One who is so listened to, who is said dwells in the inner person, namely Christ, that is the unchangeable power and eternal Wisdom of God.[7]

On the Teacher claims that ideas are learned by one human from another through the use of the manipulation of sound waves by tongues, teeth, and lips only because the inward Teacher allows sensible symbols to transmit the universal ideas. But something other than a Platonic language theory is at play; there is also the necessary consideration of the nature of time. The Wisdom of God is eternal, yet the Wisdom dwells within the mind and teaches the temporal creature in time. When teaching occurs, it occurs because the Eternal God acts in the Moment and grabs the student by the hair. Augustine explains that it is because of God's ability to act in such a moment that often students fail to see the act as one of the Eternal God and attribute the idea to a temporal teacher.

> People are wrong when they call those teachers who are not. But because very often there is no interval between the moment of speaking and the moment of knowing, and because they inwardly learn immediately after the speaker has given his admonition, they suppose that they have been taught in an external fashion by him who gave the admonition.[8]

The fascination with this ability of the Eternal God to interact with temporal human minds fills Augustine's famous chapter eleven in the *Confessions*.

6. Kierkegaard, *Philosophical Fragments*, 43.

7. Augustine, *On the Teacher* XI.36,95. My translation of the Latin pronouns for God are used.

8. Augustine, *On the Teacher* XIV. 45,100.

Section V—Temporal Moments: Teaching in Time

And the paradox presented occupies the majority of Kierkegaard's *Philosophical Fragments*. Climacus considers the Moment when the student sees the new idea. In the Moment, the student sees more than simply that she is in error. No doubt Socrates could have easily shown her this. But when real learning occurs, a new insight happens. The student is transformed from a creature in error into a creature without this error. She does not simply understand herself as she is; she has been transformed and made new.

In order to understand this ontological change, according to Kierkegaard's Climacus, we must have a new understanding of teaching. The teaching Moment is not one of recognition but one of transformation. The human teacher does not just open up the memory of the student nor point out to the student how little she knows. The human teacher and the student are, in the Moment of the lesson, a vehicle for the Teacher to break through and transform both into new creations.

> But when the God becomes a Teacher, his love cannot be merely seconding and assisting, but is creative, giving a new being to the learner, or as we have called him, the man born anew; by which designation we signify the transition from non-being to being.[9]

Kierkegaard's point is that all is not vanity after all. New insights are possible. New insights are given from the Eternal to the temporal creature in time. Solomon is wrong, there are infinitely new things under the sun.

At this point a question might emerge, a question that strains human consciousness' ability to handle paradox. If teachers and students change in time, does the Teacher also change? If God is eternal, the answer seems to be no. But God's relationship with temporal creatures is essential to Christian epistemology. Is God affected by these relationships with students in time? Years after taking Brague's class on Aristotle I saw him at a conference about Christian philosophy. Discussing *Kairos* in a Christian context, someone asked him if there is change in Heaven, if God also becomes new. Brague's answer was simple, "If we want to know if there is change in Heaven, I guess, we will just have to wait and see." Whatever the nature of God, our nature now is temporal. We are creatures who wait and then see.

The temporality is essential to human consciousness. Unlike Plato's Socrates, and unlike Linklater's Jesse, Kierkegaard's Climacus insists that human consciousness is a temporal thing. Insight, if it is known, is only known in time. The moment of the insight into the Eternal is temporal.

---

9. Kierkegaard, *Philosophical Fragments*, 38.

> When does he receive the condition? In the Moment... He receives accordingly the eternal condition in the Moment, and is aware that he has so received it; for otherwise he merely comes to himself in the consciousness that he had it from eternity. It is in the Moment that he receives it, and from the Teacher himself.[10]

LESSONS FOR THE TEMPORAL TEACHER

Socrates taught that the excellent teacher only awakens the temporal mind to the Eternal. Aristotle taught that the virtuous teacher grabs the Moment in the right way so that the student might learn properly how to make the most of each occasion. Kierkegaard and Augustine claim that the human teacher teaches the student in the Moment which is opened by the Eternal God. In the Moment of teaching, the student and the teacher are made new. When the student, or the teacher, forgets and then later recollects the Moment of the lesson, she is, yet again, made new. For the human, conscious awareness is always and only occurring in time. Learning, whether by recollection or by recognition, is always a real change that occurs in time. This view has several ramifications for the actual practical art of teaching.

First, of course, Socratic humility is required. The teacher remembers she is not the Teacher, but a teacher, an occasion for the student. It is not her insight that the student learns but the Insight. And the student is her occasion as well. Thus, in a moment of teaching it may well be the teacher who learns and is made new rather than the student. As such the student is to be viewed as a gift. The teacher also remembers that she does not create the moment of insight, nor grab the Moment's ponytail in order to make it serve her purpose of teaching. Rather, the teacher recognizes that the Moment is created by the God. In the Moment, the teacher and the student are pulled by the hair and stopped short so as to see clearly the new insight. Thus the temporal moment, like the student, is not to be considered a burden nor an opportunity, but a Gift.

Second, attentiveness is demanded. To believe that the classroom and the students that inhabit it are Gifts is to be humble, but it is also to be hopeful and alert. To believe that insight is possible is to hold hope in each moment that this might be the Moment in which one is changed from error into insight. Such hopefulness wakes up the slumbering mind of the professor who might be bored by a Sisyphean view of teaching. Insight is

---

10. Kierkegaard, *Philosophical Fragments*, 79.

Section V—Temporal Moments: Teaching in Time

possible. New transformations occur. A teacher who believes this, who has faith in this possibility, expects the Gift of the Insight in the Moment of teaching each student. She is alert. She rushes to class to be on time. She is excited to be in this time with the students. She lacks a resentful sense of duty. She is alert and attentive like the bridesmaids in the parable; she holds her lantern, trims the wick, keeps the oil jars full.

Third, there is an appreciation for time's flow. Too often, a Platonic view of time and eternity, not only dulls a professor's sharpness but dampens her ability for joy. Perhaps the teacher did tell a similar joke a decade earlier, and perhaps the idea is not so new after all, but in the Moment the joke is humorous and the idea is fresh. And as temporal creatures, we live in moments. To fail to appreciate moments even as they pass by is to fail to appreciate the nature of human life and thought itself. Appreciation of the Moment, the ability to experience joy now, keeps one from lethargy, boredom, and vanity. It allows us, not to make better use of time but to expect more in time. It allows us to be something other than the people Jesse and Celine deplore in *Before Sunrise*. Jesse says,

> You know what drives me crazy? It's all these people talking about how great technology is, and how it saves all this time. But, what good is saved time, if nobody uses it? If it just turns into more busy work. You never hear somebody say, 'With the time I've saved by using my word processor, I'm gonna go to a Zen monastery and hang out'. I mean, you never hear that.[11]

Jim Conlon has never been someone who tries to save time, but rather a teacher who values time. He has taken advantage of the occasions given him and taught his colleagues and students to appreciate the moment. Let us all, in time, learn from his philosophy of presence in order to become better teachers and students.

BIBLIOGRAPHY

Augustine. "On the Teacher." In *Augustine Earlier Writings*. Translated by J.H.S. Burleigh. Philadelphia: Westminster, 1953.
Kierkegaard, Soren. *Philosophical Fragments*. Translated by David Swenson and Howard Hong. Princeton: Princeton University Press, 1974
Linklater, Richard, dir. *Before Sunrise*. 1995; US; Castle Rock Entertainment. Distributed by Columbia Pictures.

11. Linklater, *Before Sunrise*.